D0295062

MODEL BUILDING TECHNIQUES FOR MANAGEMENT

Published in association with
Cranfield Institute Press

Model building techniques for management

JOHN HULL
JOHN MAPES
BRIAN WHEELER
Cranfield School of Management

SAXON  HOUSE

© John Hull, John Mapes and Brian Wheeler, 1976

All rights reserved. No part of this publication may be reproduced, stored in a retrieval system, or transmitted in any form or by any means, electronic, mechanical, photocopying, recording, or otherwise without the prior permission of Teakfield Limited.

First published in Great Britain, 1976 by SAXON HOUSE,
Teakfield Limited, Westmead, Farnborough, Hampshire, England

Second Impression 1977
Third Impression 1978

ISBN 0 566 00149 7

Printed in Great Britain by Biddles Limited, Guildford, Surrey

Contents

List of tables

List of figures

Preface

Books in the model building/operational research area have a tendency to fall into one of two fairly distinct categories. Either they are short introductions to the subject for the manager who wants to know what operational research is but does not want to get involved in any of the details, or they are comprehensive textbooks suitable only for the practitioner. As teachers of management we have found this a little unsatisfactory. Nowadays it is not sufficient for a manager merely to know what operational research is. He must be able to recognise those problems which would benefit from the assistance of an operational research specialist and then be able to work in partnership with the specialist while the problems are being solved. This book will, we believe, enable him to do this.

'Model Building Techniques for Management' has been developed from the material which we use on management courses at Cranfield. In particular it is the basis of some of the quantitative analysis lectures on the master's degree in business administration. Students of this course have an average age of twenty-nine and at least four years' industrial experience. Most of the students are practising managers who have taken a year off from their jobs in order to learn how to manage better. They are not interested in academic theory. Their primary objective is to learn practical skills and techniques which will enable them to do their job better when they return to industry or commerce. The reader will therefore find that no advanced mathematical or statistical concepts have been used in this book. The topics selected for inclusion are those areas of operational research which have been found the most useful and profitable when applied to business problems.

Chapter 1 provides a general introduction to operational research and to the steps in carrying out an operational research investigation. Chapter 2 is about the types of models which are used in operational research and the methods of analysis available. Chapter 3 looks at resource allocation, one of the most successful areas of application for operational research. The technique of linear programming is described with attention being concentrated on problem formulation and the interpretation of results. Chapter 4 describes forecasting techniques – particularly short term forecasting techniques. Chapter 5 is about simulation, one of the most powerful tools available for comparing the effects of alternative operating conditions. Chapter 6 covers decision analysis, a method for improving the quality of decision making by portraying complex decisions in the form of decision trees and comparing alternative courses of action by means of objective quantitative criteria. Finally Chapter 7 summarises some of the difficulties of using models and outlines ways in which a manager can ensure the successful introduction of operational research into his organisation.

At the end of Chapters 3, 4, 5 and 6 there are exercises to enable the reader to test his understanding of the material covered. To gain full benefit from the book the reader should attempt all of these. Five case studies are also included and an analysis of these should enable the reader to gain a feel for some of the problems which are encountered when models are used in practice.

Finally we would like to express our thanks to all our friends at Cranfield and elsewhere who have assisted in the preparation of this book, in particular to Linda Thompson who typed several drafts of the entire script and Lois Knibbs who prepared the diagrams.

John Hull
John Mapes
Brian Wheeler

1 Introduction

Many top managers – although well informed about functions such as personnel, management accounting and market research – disclaim any knowledge of operational research (or management science as it is sometimes called) and treat it as a subject which is best left entirely to the specialist. This is a pity. Operational research like all other business activities needs to be subject to strict management controls. These controls must ensure first that the operational research effort is being directed towards the right area of the business and second that it is cost-effective. They cannot do this successfully unless the person exercising the controls has some knowledge of the true nature of the operational research activity.

This book has been designed as an introduction to operational research for those managers who would describe themselves as non-mathematical. Its aim is to demonstrate that although the non-specialist cannot understand all the ins and outs of the subject he can understand sufficient of them to be able to play a full part in influencing what the specialist does and how he does it.

Briefly, operational research can be described as a scientific approach to managerial decision making. It attempts to quantify the consequences of the various courses of action open to the manager and to select the alternative which best meets his objectives. It was originally developed during the Second World War to assist in the solution of repetitive tactical problems (for example, it was used to determine the ideal setting on depth charges when enemy submarines were being attacked). It has now been applied to a variety of problems – both tactical and strategic – in business.

Operational research considers a business situation as a 'system' with flows of information, flows of materials and flows of money. It recognises that the system reacts in certain ways to internal and external events and aims to quantify the relationships between the elements in the system so as to reach conclusions about the way in which the system should be operated. Of course it must be admitted at the outset of this book that operational research does not – and should not – always have the last word about the way in which a system is operated. Often factors are present which are difficult to quantify but which need to be taken into account before a final decision is reached. The manager must then use his judgement to balance the quantitative results from operational research against these less tangible factors.

The scientific method

We have said that operational research is a scientific approach to management problem solving. Let us first consider what the classical scientific approach involves and see how applicable this approach is to the solution of management problems.

The steps in the scientific method are usually listed as follows: (a) recognition of problem; (b) formulation of problem; (c) formulation of a hypothesis; (d) experimentation; (e) modification of hypothesis; (f) further experimentation; (g) verification of hypothesis. For example, a chemist when carrying out a routine reaction might discover traces of an impurity in the final product. After checking the purity of his raw materials and verifying the precise conditions under which the impurity appears he might decide that the impurity is the product of a subsidiary reaction. The problem would then be formulated as the determination of the nature of this subsidiary reaction. The chemist would formulate a hypothesis concerning the mechanism by which the reaction occurs and devise experiments to test this hypothesis. From the results of his experiments he would modify the hypothesis carrying out further experimentation until, finally, he arrived at a hypothesis consistent with the experimental data.

Now let us look at a typical management problem. A production manager observes that long queues of machine operators regularly build up at the tool-room. While the operators are queueing up for tools and materials their machines are idle, incurring high costs in lost production time. The production manager decides that his problem is to determine the number of tool-room attendants which will minimise tool-room operating costs plus the cost of machine down-time.

The classical scientific approach to this problem would be to experiment. The tool-room would be operated for a representative period with varying numbers of attendants and the queues which built up observed. However, the approach would involve a number of practical difficulties:

(a) the experiment would take a long time;
(b) conditions would be liable to vary during the experiment so that it might be difficult to separate the effect of number of attendants on queue size from other factors; and

(c) extra staff would have to be recruited for the experiment. Possibly these would have to be redeployed later.

(Other managerial problems could give rise to even more difficulties than these. Imagine using experimentation to evaluate various factory sizes!)

Operational research overcomes these difficulties by the use of what are termed models. Briefly, a model in a given situation is any representation of the system under consideration. A map of a town, a scale model of a new building, a financial balance sheet and a mathematical equation are all examples of models. If the model includes all the relevant features of the system then the behaviour of the model can be used to predict the behaviour of the system. This means that the operational researcher need not experiment with the real world; he can instead experiment with a model of the real world.

In the tool-room problem the model used might be a mathematical equation showing how queue length depends on the number of tool-room attendants, average service time per customer and average number of customer arrivals per minute. This model could be used to estimate average queue length for varying numbers of attendants. This information might in turn be used in a costing model relating total costs to average queue length, number of tool-room attendants, labour costs and machine down-time costs.

The operational research methodology

We can now list the steps in operational research methodology.

    1 Recognise the problem.
    2 Formulate the problem.
    3 Construct suitable model.
    4 Use the model to solve the problem.
    5 Implement solution.

1   Recognise the problem

This step may not involve the operational researcher at all. A manager may decide that the results achieved by his organisation could be improved upon or he may have been set objectives which cannot be achieved using present methods of operation and resource constraints. There is no systematic approach to the recognition of problem areas although some companies find check lists of typical symptoms a useful basis for selecting problems for investigation. In the main it is up to the individual manager to keep up to date on the performance and methods of operation of comparable organisations in order to recognise areas where the performance of his own organisation could be improved.

2 Formulate the problem

Correct formulation of the problem is a very important part of any operational research investigation, and it is frequently the most difficult part. Often it is only after a substantial amount of data has been collected that the real problem can be recognised. It is therefore necessary to modify the formulation of the problem from time to time as the investigation progresses. One investigation was initially concerned with the determination of the correct size of a warehouse which was to be built to hold stocks of a chemical which was sold in a variety of grades. It rapidly became clear that the scope of the investigation would need to be extended to include the method of scheduling batches of material during the manufacturing process. Eventually the analysis showed that it was possible to reduce considerably the range of grades stocked and to improve forward planning so that more large orders could be manufactured for direct shipment to customers. As a result of these changes it was possible to reduce the level of total stocks held so that construction of a new warehouse was not necessary.

An important aspect of formulation is the setting of appropriate objectives. In a lot of cases the objective can be simply defined in terms of reducing costs or increasing profitability. In other cases the objective may be to reduce absenteeism or to increase machine utilisation. Sometimes it will not be possible to define the problem in terms of a single objective. The investigator may be asked to reduce total costs, to increase the level of service to the customer and to reduce staff turnover. Such multiple objective problems are much more difficult to formulate adequately. Sometimes, however, the decision maker is able to define a primary objective and then specify acceptable levels for the secondary objectives. For example, the investigator may be asked to obtain the minimum cost solution which will provide a given customer service level and ensure that staff turnover is below a specified level.

3 Construct suitable model

There is a considerable art to the construction of models of business systems. The model should not be over-complicated, but it must contain sufficient variables to give a realistic representation of the behaviour of the real system.

The preliminary step is usually to gain an understanding of the system to be modelled. The operational researcher will do this by talking to people concerned in the running of the system and collecting data on its operation. Eventually he will be able to construct a logical model of the system showing the important variables and the ways in which they are likely to be inter-related. For example, in a certain situation labour turnover might be considered an important factor in the model, and the probability of an individual resigning during a specified period might be thought to depend on age, length of service, sex, job category and the general level of employment.

Having established the logical model of the system it is necessary to establish the numerical relationships between the variables and hence develop a quantitative model of the system. This usually requires a considerable amount of analysis of the statistical data available and a number of assumptions have to be made. It is important that these assumptions are clearly stated and understood as they may need to be modified later in the investigation as more information becomes available.

At this stage the investigator should have a clear statement of the objective of the investigation, preferably expressed in quantitative terms. There should be a list of the key factors which have been included in the model and a list of the factors which have been left out of the model with the reasons for their exclusion. There should also be a list of the major assumptions made. Finally there should be the model itself, a clear description of the quantitative inter-relationships between the key variables.

4 Use the model to solve the problem

The construction of a realistic model of the system being investigated is of no practical use to the decision maker unless the model can be used to solve the original problem. The major part of this book is devoted to the various methods of solution available.

5 Implement solution

Any solution to a problem, however elegant, is only of practical value after it has been implemented and the predicted benefits have been achieved. Sometimes implementation will be carried out by the manager who will operate the system rather than the operational researcher. However, the operational researcher must still take full account of the problems of implementation in reaching his solution.

In order to overcome initial resistance and to ensure that the new system is correctly operated it is important that the system and the reasons for its introduction are fully understood by everyone. In a number of cases a theoretically optimum and highly complex solution will have to be passed over in favour of a simpler one involving slightly higher costs but with a greater chance of being correctly operated by the staff concerned.

An example of the sort of problem which can arise occurred during the implementation of a new stock control system. The percentage of customers' orders which could be met directly off the warehouse shelves had been very low, about 60 per cent. A new computerised stock control system was introduced to correct this and over a period of a few months this percentage steadily increased until it reached the predicted level of 93 per cent. Unfortunately it then steadily reduced again until it was once more 60 per cent and still falling. The operational research team were called back in and they found that the problem was simply one of lack of familiarity with computers. Frequently orders were received from customers with the part numbers mistyped. The computer of course immediately rejected them. The warehousemen would recognise what the part number should be, correct the documentation by hand and send off the order. What they did not do, however, was to feed the corrected information back to the computer so that its stock records could be updated. Thus, although the computer's internal records indicated that 93 per cent of customers' orders were being met directly off the shelves, the actual service level was much lower than this. It was simple enough to alter the system to ensure that the computer received information on all stock movements but it was not a problem that the operational research team had been able to foresee.

This also highlights another aspect of implementation, the need for control to ensure that the new system is operating satisfactorily. A new system should always be regularly monitored to determine whether the forecast results are being achieved and the procedures laid down are being adhered to. If it is found that they are, no further action need be taken. If not, the situation should be investigated. It may be that there are unforeseen practical problems or that some of the assumptions made are not valid.

References

Ackoff, R.L. and Rivett, P., *A Manager's Guide to Operations Research,* Wiley, 1963.
Duckworth, E., *A Guide to Operational Research,* Methuen, 1965.
Rivett, P., *Concepts of Operational Research,* C.A. Watts, 1968.

2 Quantitative models

In the previous chapter we looked at the operational research approach to problem solving and saw that a central feature of that approach was the use of models as a basis for investigating the behaviour of a real system. In this chapter we shall look in more detail at the various types of models available and the ways in which they can be manipulated in order to solve management problems.

Types of models

Iconic models

When the word model is used in everyday conversation it is nearly always in reference to an iconic model. An iconic model is a physical representation of certain characteristics of the real system. Photographs, statues and scale models are all examples of iconic models.

Method study engineers frequently make use of iconic models when tackling office and factory layout problems. Using a plan of the area to be laid out and wooden models of the machines and other equipment to be located in the area the method study engineer can rapidly compare a large number of different layouts. However, iconic models have only a limited application to business problems as many of the important characteristics of a business system such as cash flows and flows of information do not have a physical representation.

Graphical models

There can be few managers who have not used graphical models as a convenient abstraction of reality, although most managers would not express what they were doing in model building terms.

A very simple example of a graphical model is the breakeven chart. Consider a production supervisor who has available an automatic machine and a semi-automatic machine for the manufacture of components. The automatic machine has a set up cost of £40·00 per batch and a variable cost of £0·40 per unit produced. The semi-automatic machine has a set up cost of £10·00 per batch and a variable cost of £0·50 per unit produced. The supervisor wishes to know how large a batch must be before it is

7

cheaper to use the automatic machine. This can be determined by plotting the relationship between total cost and batch size graphically for each machine. (See Figure 2.1.)

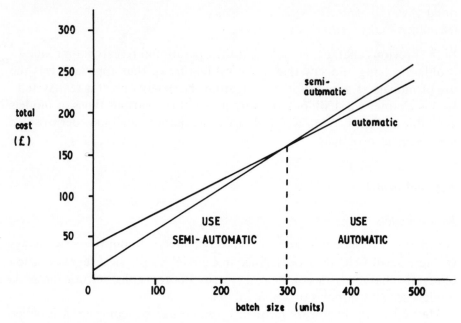

Fig. 2.1 A breakeven chart

Figure 2.1 shows that the semi-automatic machine is more economical for batches up to 300 units and the automatic machine is more economical for batches of more than 300 units.

Analogue models

An analogue model is one in which certain aspects of the behaviour of the real system are reproduced in a different medium. Graphical models are a particular type of analogue model. A popular form of analogue model involves the use of flows of electricity as an analogue for flows of material or information in a system. Such models are expensive to construct so that they are only feasible for applications where the model will be used on a regular basis for planning purposes.

Mathematical models

The most generally useful type of model is a mathematical model in which the relationships between the variables in the system are represented algebraically. As a very simple illustration of how such a model can be constructed, consider a manager in charge of a chain of petrol stations wondering whether a certain site is suitable for future expansion. Suppose that the site is on the east side of a main road (see Figure 2.2). The first thing that the manager would probably notice is the fact that vehicles travelling south could enter a garage on this site fairly easily while those travelling north would have to make a right turn across a southbound stream of traffic. He would probably wish to assume that the proportion of southbound vehicles entering the station will be different from the proportion of northbound vehicles which do so. Suppose we use the following notation:

p = proportion of southbound vehicles entering station
q = proportion of northbound vehicles entering station
V = the number of vehicles entering the station per day
S = the traffic flow on the same side of the road as the petrol station (vehicles per day)
N = the traffic flow on the opposite side of the road to the petrol station (vehicles per day)

Then a model of the situation is as follows:

$$V = pS + qN$$

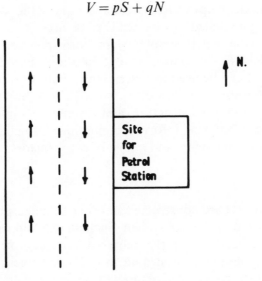

Fig. 2.2   Site for proposed petrol station

If the further assumption, that p and q are roughly constant for the type of road under consideration, is made, this model could be analysed by collecting data. S and N could be measured fairly accurately for the proposed site by observing the cars passing in both directions over a period of time. p and q could be estimated from data collected for petrol stations already in existence on roads similar to the one in Figure 2.2. V could then be related to revenue from the sales of petrol and the economic viability of the proposed site could be assessed.

Whether it is reasonable to assume in the model that p and q are roughly constant for the type of road under consideration must, of course, be determined from the data once it has been collected. (This is known as validating the model.) If the assumption proved to be inappropriate then a more complicated model, incorporating such aspects of the situation as the fact that not all garages charge the same price for petrol, is likely to be required.

The use of models

There are three main reasons for constructing a model: 1 description, 2 prediction, 3 analysis.

1 Description

A descriptive model helps us to understand rapidly the salient features of the system being modelled. If a model is to be used purely for descriptive purposes it can be much simpler than corresponding predictive and analytical models. For example, an organisation chart is a typical descriptive model. It can be used to determine rapidly who reports to whom in a large organisation. If, however, we wish to estimate the effects of altering the organisational structure, a much more complex model would be necessary, incorporating informal communication channels, the competence of existing managers and a host of other factors.

2 Prediction

A number of models are constructed in order to make predictions about the future behaviour of the real system. Such models will vary considerably in complexity depending on the required accuracy of the prediction. Graphical extrapolation of past data in order to forecast future sales is an example of a simple predictive model.

3 Analysis

Usually the model builder wishes to manipulate the model in order to determine the best method of achieving specified objectives. Clearly, use of a model for this purpose will still involve elements of description and prediction but it will also require a greater understanding of the inter-relationships between the variables in the model.

A simple financial model

With the increasing availability of computer time it should be noted that one reason for building a model is often simply to test out a number of alternatives. To illustrate this, the following are a few of the equations from a simple financial planning model which was recently built for a small company (for a full description of the model see Hull and Alexander in the references):

$$PTP_n = C_n - O_n - D_n + I_n$$
$$TP_n = PTP_n + D_n - CE_n$$
$$T_n = TD_{n-2}$$

where
    PTP_n is the pre-tax profit in year n
    C_n is the contribution in year n
    O_n is the overheads in year n
    D_n is the depreciation in year n
    I_n is the interest received in year n
    CE_n is the capital expenditure in year n
    T_n is the tax paid in year n
    TD_n is the tax due in year n
    TP_n is the taxable profit in year n

Once the model, which involved over twenty equations in total, had been encoded in an appropriate computer language is was possible to test the effect on variables such as net cash flow and cash balance of a variety of different assumptions concerning future sales levels, the rate of inflation, the rate of taxation etc. It would, to say the least, have been tedious to do the same thing without a computer model.

Deterministic and probabilistic models

A useful distinction can be made in model building between deterministic and probabilistic models. A deterministic model assumes that the values of all variables are either known exactly or can be predicted exactly; a probabilistic model, on the other hand, recognises that the values of some variables are uncertain and deals with this, using concepts from probability theory.

The problem of deciding the minimum distance route starting from a given point, visiting each of a set of specified points once and returning to the starting point, can be handled using a deterministic model. It is usually referred to as the travelling salesman problem. No probabilistic elements are involved as the locations of the points to be visited can be defined precisely and the exact distance by road between any two points can be calculated.

If we were interested in investigating the salesman's travelling time rather than the distance he travels then of course a probabilistic model might be required, as the travelling time between any two points is likely to be subject to random variations.

Most business systems have a probabilistic element. Unfortunately, with probabilistic models a considerable amount of data must be collected in order to determine each probability distribution and the analysis of models involving probability distributions is much more complicated. For these reasons a probabilistic system will often be represented by a deterministic model, each variable being given its average value. For example, the time minimisation travelling salesman problem could be treated deterministically by using the average travelling time between each pair of points and ignoring the effect of variations in journey times.

In some cases, however, it can be very misleading to use a deterministic model to represent a stochastic system. Suppose that a machine operator is controlling three machines, that the average machine cycle time is four minutes and that the average time to unload the completed part and reload the machine is two minutes. Treated deterministically it would seem that each machine will produce a part every six minutes on average. In practice both the running time and servicing time will vary about their respective averages. This will mean that machines will frequently complete their run before the operator has completed servicing the previous machine and will have to wait for attention. The average time for each machine to produce a part will therefore be greater than six minutes. In order to estimate how much greater, we would need to take into account the variability of running times and servicing times using a probabilistic model.

Methods of solution

Although a model may be constructed purely for descriptive purposes, in management a model is usually constructed in order to solve a particular problem. After constructing and validating the model it is necessary to manipulate the model in some way in order to obtain a solution of the original problem. Four main methods of analysis are important:

1 Analytical methods

In some cases a solution can be obtained using the standard algebraic/analytical procedures of mathematics. This approach can be illustrated by the derivation of the well known economic order quantity (EOQ) formula.

Suppose a company has to decide how often to order a certain component used in its manufacturing operations from a supplier. If the company orders frequently then the administrative costs of processing the orders and checking the incoming material will be high. On the other hand if the company orders relatively infrequently then money will be tied up in stock which could be used for other profit earning purposes. Suppose the company estimates:

D = its demand (units per year) for the item (assumed to be roughly constant)

C_1 = the cost of placing an order (£)

C_2 = the cost of holding one unit in stock (£) per year.

(C_2, which will be referred to as the stockholding cost, must be measured in terms of the other uses to which the money tied up in stock can be put.)

Suppose the company orders in batches of size Q. The component will have to be ordered D/Q times per year. The total (administrative) costs of placing these orders will be: $(D/Q)C_1$.

The stock held will vary between Q and 0 averaging $Q/2$. (This assumes that each batch arrives just as the old stock is running out.) The total stockholding costs incurred per year will therefore be: $(Q/2)C_2$ and the total of all the costs incurred in a year can be expressed as:

$$\frac{QC_2}{2} + \frac{DC_1}{Q}$$

A graph of the relationship between the total costs and Q has the general form shown by the continuous line in Figure 2.3 and a further analysis can be carried out to show that the least total cost (i.e. the cost corresponding to the lowest point on the curve) is given when:

$$Q = \sqrt{\frac{2DC_1}{C_2}}$$

Although the economic order quantity formula is used by a large number of organisations it is based on a model which is a considerable simplification of reality. It ignores the effects of bulk discounts, the effects on costs of ordering a number of different items at the same time and a number of other factors. Of course, if these other factors are incorporated in the model it is unlikely that the problem will be soluble by analytical methods.

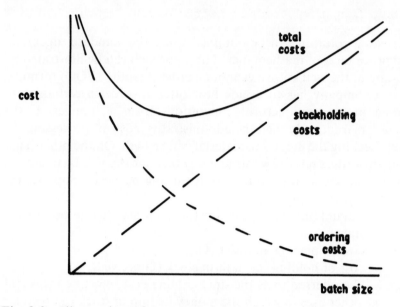

Fig. 2.3   Illustration of economic batch size formula

This highlights one of the difficulties of using analytical methods. They are usually only applicable if a number of simplifications and assumptions are made. It is often very tempting to make these assumptions, as analytical methods give precise solutions. However, it must always be borne in mind that an exact solution to the approximate problem is not necessarily the same as an approximate solution to the exact problem.

2   Use of algorithms

Algorithms are precisely defined procedures for performing calculations. They include a number of step by step procedures for determining the optimum values of the variables in certain types of models. Usually an initial set of values for the variables is chosen first. A systematic procedure is then carried out to determine whether these can be improved upon. If they can, a new set of values is calculated and the systematic procedure is repeated. If they cannot be improved upon, the optimum solution has been reached.

3   Use of heuristics

Heuristics are 'rule of thumb' procedures which produce near optimum solutions once the model has been built. Often a great deal of what is commonly termed 'trial and error' is involved. As a simple example, let us return to the travelling salesman problem which involved the minimum

14

distance route from a depot round a number of delivery points and back to the depot. A simple heuristic (clearly open to some improvement) would be: go first to the delivery point nearest to the depot and then continue by going at each stage to the delivery point which, of those not already visited, is nearest the van's current position.

4 Use of simulation

In cases where the model is complex it is usually not possible to apply any of the above methods without considerable simplification to the model. It is then usually necessary to simulate the behaviour of the real system for each of the alternative solutions under consideration.

Simulation could be used to determine the number of tills necessary in a supermarket. A suitable model having been constructed, the operation of the supermarket could be simulated for a representative period with the existing number of tills. A comparison of the simulation results with what happens in practice provides a check that the simulation is realistic. The simulation could then be repeated a number of times with varying numbers of tills. From the results the number of tills giving maximum profitability could be determined.

Simulation is not an optimising technique. It can only indicate the best of the set of alternatives which have been simulated. However, its great strength is its ability to handle very complex models without the need for simplification. Simulation does involve a lot of tedious and repetitive calculations, but these are usually carried out by computer.

Chapter 5 provides a much more detailed discussion of simulation.

References

Ackoff, R.L. and Sasieni, M.W., *Fundamentals of Operations Research,* Wiley, 1968.
Battersby, A., *Mathematics in Management,* Penguin, 1962.
Churchman, C.W., Ackoff, R.L. and Arnoff, E.L., *Introduction to Operations Research,* Wiley, 1957.
Hull, J.C. and Alexander, W., 'The Impact of Inflation on Corporate Financial Performance' *Management Decision,* vol. 14, no. 1, 1976.
Makower, M.S. and Williamson, E., *Operational Research,* English Universities Press, 1967.
Rivett, P., *Principles of Model Building,* Wiley, 1972.
Wagner, H.M., *Principles of Management Science with Applications to Executive Decisions,* Prentice-Hall, 1970.

Case A   Hopkins Supplies Ltd

Hopkins Supplies Ltd have been established as builders' merchants for about twenty-five years. In that time the business has grown from being a one man organisation operated from a small warehouse in a back street in North London to a national concern with eight different sales regions, each with its own warehouse facilities, clerical staff and sales force.

'Hops' (as the business is known in the trade) does not operate in quite the same way as most builders' merchants. Selected building materials such as plywood, plasterboard, copper tubes, roofing felt, etc., are bought in bulk from a number of different manufacturers, stocked in the eight regional warehouses and sold by personal visits of Hops' salesmen to building contractors in all parts of the UK. Like most distributors, Hops deals with customers who buy the goods in relatively small quantities. Large national building contractors who can order in bulk tend to negotiate directly with the manufacturer.

Each region has its own sales force of one or two men. Each of these salesmen handles about a hundred accounts and spends about 70 per cent of his time in the field. The prices charged by Hops to the contractor are not fixed. The salesmen themselves negotiate the best price they can, using their own knowledge of the market and the pricing policies of their chief competitors to guide them. A considerable part of the income of each salesman is a commission based on both the value of the sales he makes and the mark-up (profit margin as a percentage of selling price) that he achieves.

Until recently it seemed that nothing could stop Hops. The firm weathered successive periods of expansion and contraction in the building trade, managing at the same time to take advantage of a number of valuable expansion opportunities itself. Then, about a year ago, with a sudden increase in building activity, many new firms entered the market. First the pressure was on delivery; now it is on price. In order to earn any commission at all Hops salesmen are being forced to cut mark-ups to less than half their previous level.

George Hopkins is worried. In the good old days mark-ups averaged over 40 per cent and the business looked highly profitable, however the accounts were presented. Now, with lower profit margins, tighter controls must, he knows, be kept on the salesmen. With this in mind, two months ago he asked for a complete breakdown and analysis of all operating costs. The report he received (see Exhibit 1) confirmed his worst fears. With clerical, warehousing, distribution and selling costs split correctly between the invoices, nearly 50 per cent of the orders currently being negotiated by his salesmen can be seen to be unprofitable.

The trouble is that a simple directive to his salesmen such as 'Keep mark-ups above 20 per cent' does not work. The analysis shows that on a big order for a high priced line 15 per cent can be a sufficient mark-up, whereas on a small order for a low priced line 25 per cent is often not enough to cover operating costs. Hops carry 20,000 lines in ten different product categories. The salesman cannot be given detailed instructions on how to proceed in every given situation – that would require a thirty lb. price book and, apart from anything else, the salesman would be laughed out of the customer's office! On the other hand he could not expect the salesmen to be supermen working out all the clerical, warehousing, distribution and selling costs in their heads. The salesmen were very good at juggling cost price, selling prices and mark-ups in their heads, but a complicated costing like that in the report would be completely beyond them.

Assignment

Formulate a set of equations describing this situation and consider how it might be useful to George Hopkins.

Exhibit 1
Costing report: Hopkins Supplies Ltd

In this report we have considered how the company's operating costs (i.e. all costs except fixed administrative overhead costs) should be allocated between invoices. The costs can be conveniently divided into four categories: (i) clerical costs, (ii) warehouse costs, (iii) distribution costs, (iv) selling costs.

Clerical costs (i.e. invoicing, stock withdrawals etc.) depend on the number of different lines on an invoice and we estimate them to be £0·50 per line per invoice.

Warehouse costs (i.e. stockholding costs, handling costs etc.) depend on the cost price of the lines on the invoice, but should be charged at different rates for lines in different product categories to take account of wide variations in the stock turns achieved. Table 1 summarises our findings.

Distribution costs (i.e. transporting goods from warehouse to customer) should be allocated on the basis of cost price, as total cost price of goods carried is the criterion used by the company in determining lorry loads.

Table 1

Product category	1	2	3	4	5	6	7	8	9	10
Warehouse costs as a fraction of cost price	0·04	0·02	0·08	0·08	0·01	0·12	0·01	0·12	0·20	0·08

Our analysis shows that distribution costs currently amount to 6 per cent of cost price.

Selling costs consist mainly of salesmen's commission. They should be allocated on the basis of profit margin, as this is the main determinant of the commission. Our analysis shows that selling costs are currently 10 per cent of the profit margin for all product categories.

To illustrate the above we will cost out a typical invoice.

Table 2

	Product category	Unit cost price	Total cost price	Selling price
400 vinyl floor tiles	4	0·02	8·00	10·00
10 sheets 8′ × 8″ plywood	1	2·00	20·00	23·15
1,200 1½″ screws	7	0·001	1·20	1·50
1,200 1″ screws	7	0·001	1·20	1·50
Total			30·40	36·15

Clerical costs:	$4 \times 0·50$	$= 2·00$
Warehouse costs:	$0·08 \times 8 + 0·04 \times 20 + 0·01 \times 1·20 + 0·01 \times 1·20$	$= 1·46$
Distribution costs:	$0·06 \times 30·40$	$= 1·82$
Selling costs:	$0·10 \times 5·75$	$= 0·57$
Total costs:		$5·85$

The profit margins negotiated by the salesmen on the above invoice are therefore inadequate to cover the company's operating costs. Our analysis reveals that 48 per cent of all invoices are similar to the one above in this respect.

3 Linear programming

The technique of linear programming (LP) is concerned with the problem of achieving a specified objective with limited resources. This is probably the commonest of all the problems which the manager has to face. The resources may include cash, manpower, machines, vehicles and material. The objective may be the maximisation of profits, or the minimisation of costs. In either case the manager's task is to allocate his resources in the best possible way.

The importance of linear programming can be seen from the large number of completely different situations where the technique can be applied. For example:

1   In situations where certain production resources are shared by a number of products, LP can be used to answer the question: What mix of product will provide most profit?
2   In situations where certain amounts of a commodity are to be shipped from a number of warehouses, ports or mines to a number of sites or customers, LP can be used to answer the question: How much should be transported along each possible route to minimise transport costs?
3   In situations where a fuel, animal feedstuff or any other mixture has to satisfy specified requirements, LP can be used to answer the question: In what proportions should raw materials be blended together in order to minimise costs?
4   In situations where a production schedule requires certain lengths of material to be cut in certain widths and where the material is only available in certain standard widths, LP can be used to answer the question: How should the material be cut so as to minimise wastage?
5   In situations where certain production deadlines must be met and where costs are attached to working overtime and holding stocks, LP can be used to produce a minimum cost production plan.

The precise conditions necessary for the application of linear programming will be given later, but at this stage the following points are worth noting:

1   There must be a number of variables whose values are to be determined.

2 There must be restrictions on the values the variables can take. (We shall use the following symbols: $\leqslant$ to mean 'must be less than or equal to'; $\geqslant$ to mean 'must be greater than or equal to'; $=$ to mean 'must be equal to'.) And

3 There must be an 'objective function' to be maximised or minimised.

Two-dimensional problems

Problems with only two variables can give considerable insight into the ideas behind linear programming, because with only two variables it is possible to see the relationships involved by plotting values of one of the variables on the horizontal axis of a graph and values of the other variable on the vertical axis. As an illustration, we will consider a product mix problem involving two products.

Clarion Co. Ltd consists of a foundry, a machine shop and a fitting bay. It manufactures two products, a pedestal and a bracket. Both products require a certain amount of time in the foundry, the machine shop and the fitting bay. The times used in each of these per unit of each product manufactured are given in Table 3.1.

Table 3.1

Hours required in different departments to manufacture products in Clarion Co. Ltd

Department	Hours required for pedestal	Hours required for bracket
Foundry	1	4
Machine shop	3	4
Fitting bay	4	2

The hours available per week for the manufacture of the two products are given in Table 3.2 and the contribution to overheads (which will also be referred to as the profit) from the manufacture and sale of each product is shown in Table 3.3.

We assume that there are no market constraints (i.e. that the company can sell all that it can produce), and that the company wants to know the best amounts to produce of each product in order to maximise the contribution to fixed overheads under the given conditions.

20

Table 3.2

Hours available for manufacturing different products in Clarion Co. Ltd

Department	Manufacturing hours available/week
Foundry	52
Machine shop	60
Fitting bay	60

Table 3.3

Contributions to overheads from manufacturing different products in Clarion Co. Ltd

	Pedestal	Bracket
Contribution to overheads £/unit produced	48	36

In this case it is very easy to identify the variables in the problem as: (a) the number of pedestals to be produced per week; and (b) the number of brackets to be produced per week. We shall denote the first variable by X_1 and the second by X_2.

There are a number of restrictions on the values the variables can take. These can be expressed as relationships in terms of the variables. From Tables 3.1 and 3.2 we have:

$$X_1 + 4X_2 \leqslant 52$$
$$3X_1 + 4X_2 \leqslant 60$$
$$4X_1 + 2X_2 \leqslant 60$$

Also, as the variables cannot be negative:

$$X_1 \geqslant 0$$
$$X_2 \geqslant 0$$

Looking at the contribution to overheads, we can write down the objective:

$$\text{Maximise } Z = 48X_1 + 36X_2$$

To see how these relationships can be expressed graphically, consider first the constraint relating to the foundry, i.e.

$$X_1 + 4X_2 \leqslant 52$$

If we produce no X_2 we could produce up to fifty-two units of X_1 (ignoring any other capacity limitations). On the other hand, if we produced no X_1, up to $52/4 = 13$ units of X_2 would then be possible. These possibilities

$$X_2 = 0, \quad X_1 = 52$$
and
$$X_1 = 0, \quad X_2 = 13$$

are represented by the points P and Q in Figure 3.1. Points on the line joining PQ are points which are such that:

$$X_1 + 4X_2 = 52$$

i.e. they are points where we are at the limit of the foundry constraint. The non-negative conditions exclude values of X_1 to the left of the vertical axis and values of X_2 below the horizontal axis. Therefore only points in the shaded area in Figure 3.1 represent values of X_1 and X_2 which satisfy the foundry constraint.

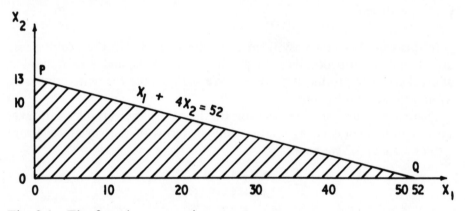

Fig. 3.1   The foundry constraint

We now have to consider the constraint imposed by hours available in the machine shop. If we consider the limiting case of this constraint we again get the equation of a straight line, i.e:

$$3X_1 + 4X_2 = 60$$

Superimposing this line on Figure 3.1, we get Figure 3.2.

Considering the machine shop alone, points representing possible values of X_1 and X_2 must lie below or up to the line representing the limit imposed by time available in the machine shop. If we consider the machine shop and the foundry together, only points which lie within the limits

22

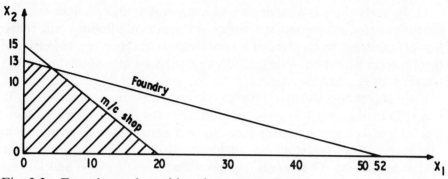

Fig. 3.2 Foundry and machine shop constraints

imposed by both are possible. It follows that the shaded area in Figure 3.2 represents pairs of values of X_1 and X_2 which lie within both constraints.

It now remains to include on the graph the third constraint, i.e.

$$4X_1 + 2X_2 \leqslant 60$$

This has been done in Figure 3.3. Only the shaded area bounded by the three lines in Figure 3.3 contains points which satisfy the conditions of all three constraints. This shaded area is called the 'feasible region'. It represents all feasible solutions, i.e. all values of variables which satisfy the conditions of the constraints. The basic problem in linear programming is that of finding the particular feasible solution which is optimal.

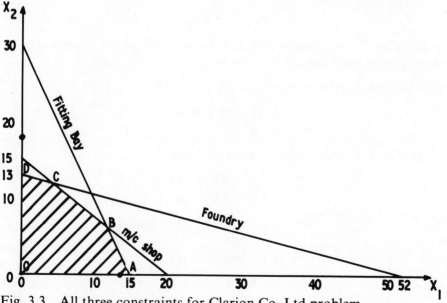

Fig. 3.3 All three constraints for Clarion Co. Ltd problem

23

Fortunately there is a theorem which states that an optimum solution can be found by looking only at a particular category of solutions called *basic feasible solutions*. In the case of a two-dimensional problem, the effect of this theorem is that an optimum solution must lie at one of the corners (vertices) of the feasible region.

If we accept this we have only to consider the corner points 0, A, B, C and D in Figure 3.3 as possible candidates for the optimum solution. The origin represents zero production and hence zero contribution to overheads. It can therefore be quickly ruled out as the location of the optimum solution. That leaves four possible points: A, B, C and D. One way of finding out which one is best is to consider each in turn.

At Point A $\qquad\qquad X_1 = 15; \ X_2 = 0$

and since the contribution to overheads is given by

$$Z = 48X_1 + 36X_2$$

it follows that the contribution to overheads (£) at A
$$= 48 \times 15 + 36 \times 0$$
$$= 720$$

Point B occurs at the intersection of the lines

$$3X_1 + 4X_2 = 60$$
$$4X_1 + 2X_2 = 60$$

i.e. at the point:

$$X_1 = 12; \ X_2 = 6$$

(this can be found either by solving the two simultaneous equations or by reading from the graph)

and the contribution to overheads (£)

$$= 48 \times 12 + 36 \times 6$$
$$= 792$$

Point C occurs at the intersection of the lines

$$X_1 + 4X_2 = 52$$
$$3X_1 + 4X_2 = 60$$

i.e. at:

$$X_1 = 4; \ X_2 = 12$$

and this gives a contribution to overheads (£)

$$= 48 \times 4 + 36 \times 12$$
$$= 624$$

Thus as we go round the perimeter of the feasible region the contribution increases from 0 to A to B. It then decreases as we go from B to C. Once the value of the objective function starts to decrease, going round the perimeter of the feasible region it will always continue to decrease. Thus the maximum contribution to overheads has now already been found as £792 at point B. To confirm this we note that at D

$$X_1 = 0; \quad X_2 = 13$$

and contribution to overheads (£)

$$= 48 \times 0 + 36 \times 13$$
$$= 468$$

Lines of iso-profit

There is another method of finding the optimum solution which sheds further light on the ideas of linear programming. This other method involves drawing lines of 'iso-profit'. These are lines drawn so that any point on the line gives the same profit (just as iso-bars represent lines of equal barometric pressure). We recall that the objective function (£) was:

$$Z = 48X_1 + 36X_2$$

Consider first the line of iso-profit for a profit of £720 (the choice of £720 is quite arbitrary). One way of obtaining this profit value is to produce only X_1 and none of X_2. In this case we would need to produce:

$$\frac{720}{48} = 15 \text{ units of } X_1$$

so $X_1 = 15; \quad X_2 = 0$ is a possible point on the £720 iso-profit line. Another alternative is to produce none of X_1 and only X_2, in which case we would need to produce

$$\frac{720}{36} = 20 \text{ units of } X_2$$

$X_1 = 0; \quad X_2 = 20$ is therefore another possible point on the £720 iso-profit line.

These two points are shown by crosses on Figure 3.4. Since the contribution is proportional to the amounts made of each product, a straight line joining these two points will give all the possible combinations of X_1 and X_2 which produce £720 contribution.

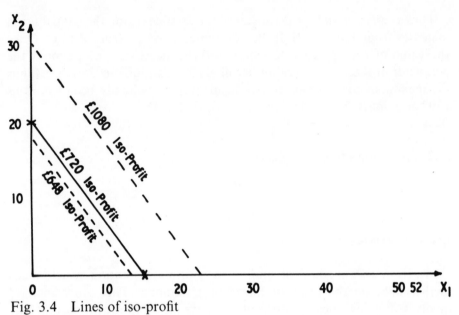

Fig. 3.4   Lines of iso-profit

Similarly we can draw iso-profit lines for other amounts. (The iso-profit lines for £1,080 and £648 are shown by dotted lines in Figure 3.4.) Notice that the lines of iso-profit are parallel to one another. Looking at Figure 3.4, we see that the further away the line of iso-profit is from the origin, the greater the profit. The next point is best demonstrated by some form of movable visual aid. The reader is asked to follow the instructions and see for himself. Put a ruler on Figure 3.3 to represent the £648 iso-profit line. This line passes through the points $X_1 = 13.5$ on the horizontal X_1 axis and $X_2 = 18$ on the vertical X_2 axis. (These two points have been marked by small dots on the axes to make them easier to find.) Now anywhere along this line, within the shaded area, represents a feasible solution giving a profit of £648. Move the ruler slightly outwards, but parallel to its original position. It now represents a new iso-profit line where the profit is greater but where less of the line is contained within the feasible region. Eventually, as the line of iso-profit is moved outwards, it happens that point B is the only point on the line which is feasible. Point B is therefore as far from the origin as we can go with a line of iso-profit while still having a feasible solution. It must therefore represent the optimal solution.

The whole situation is represented in Figure 3.5. Whatever the angle of inclination of the iso-profit lines it can easily be seen that the maximum profit must lie at one of the corners of the feasible region. (This illustrates the truth of the theorem referred to earlier.)

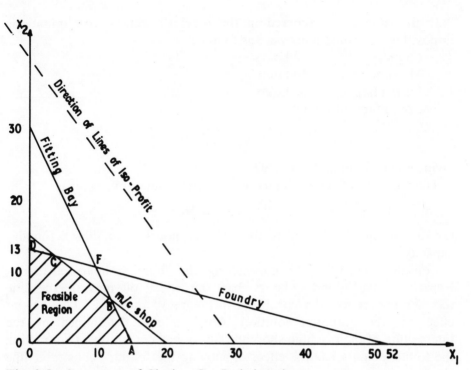

Fig. 3.5   Summary of Clarion Co. Ltd situation

To summarise: we have shown that in problems with two dimensions, i.e. two variables, an optimum solution will lie at one of the vertices. This will either be at the intersection of two constraints, as point B in Figure 3.3, or at the intersection of a constraint and one of the axes (e.g. point A). An exception occurs when the numbers in the problem happen to be such that lines of iso-profit are parallel to one of the constraints. Then there is a multiplicity of optimal solutions, with optimal solutions at two adjacent vertices. This exception is more important in theory than in practice.

Sensitivity analysis and shadow values exemplified by a two-dimensional problem

A question which frequently occurs in LP is: How much more profit or how much greater contribution to overheads can be achieved if we have more capacity in one or other of the resources? In technical terms, what change is produced in the maximum value of the objective function if we relax one of the constraints?

In the situation considered in the previous section, the limitations imposed by the constraints were as follows:

Foundry   52 hours
Machine shop   60 hours
Fitting bay   60 hours

The optimum solution was:

$$X_1 = 12$$
$$X_2 = 6$$

giving a maximum profit of £792.

The number of foundry hours used in the optimal solution was:

$$12 + 4 \times 6 = 36$$

(i.e. the optimum solution involved sixteen hours of unutilised foundry capacity).

Consider expanding or contracting the foundry hours available. Expanding the foundry hours has the effect of moving the line representing the foundry constraint in Figure 3.5 outwards. This has no effect on the optimum solution, which is still determined by the intersection of the machine shop and fitting bay constraints. Contracting the foundry hours has the effect of moving the foundry constraint line closer to the origin, and again there will be no effect on the optimum solution providing the total foundry hours available are kept above thirty-six.

Consider next changing the machine shop hours available.

Figure 3.6 shows Figure 3.5 with a new machine shop constraint line indicating that sixty-six (instead of sixty) machine shop hours are available. It is easy to see that it has the effect of moving the optimum solution from B to B'. The new values of the variables at the optimum solution are:

$$X_1 = 10 \cdot 8$$
$$X_2 = 8 \cdot 4$$

and the new contribution to overheads is:

$$48 \times 10 \cdot 8 + 36 \times 8 \cdot 4 = 820 \cdot 8 \text{ (£)}$$

Thus, increasing the machine shop hours from sixty to sixty-six (i.e. by six hours) has the effect of increasing the optimum contribution by £28·8 from £792 to £820·8.

The *shadow value* of a constraint is defined as: the rate of increase in total profit (or reduction in total cost) per unit relaxation of the constraint.

We have shown that relaxing the foundry constraint has no effect on total profit. The shadow value of the foundry constraint is therefore zero.

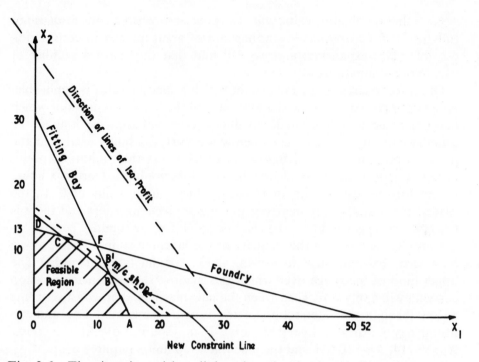

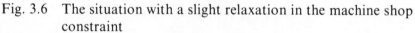

Fig. 3.6   The situation with a slight relaxation in the machine shop
constraint

The shadow value of the machine shop constraint is:

$$\frac{28\cdot8}{6} = 4\cdot8 \text{ £/hour}$$

This means that £4·8 change in contribution can be obtained per unit
increase in the limit of the machine shop constraint.

The shadow value of the fitting bay constraint can be calculated
similarly as 8·4 £/hour.

These results are summarised in Table 3.4.

Table 3.4
Shadow values of constraints in the Clarion Co. Ltd

Constraint	Capacity available (hours)	Capacity used (hours)	Shadow value of constraint (£/hour)
Foundry	52	36	0
Machine shop	60	60	4·8
Fitting bay	60	60	8·4

Note that the shadow value will always be zero when a constraint is not fully utilised. Clearly shadow values are of great interest in considering possible plant expansion, and we will find that they have a number of uses in other situations.

Of further interest is the range over which a shadow value is applicable. As an example, consider the shadow value of the foundry constraint which happens to be zero. The shadow value of zero will apply so long as the foundry capacity is not reduced below the thirty-six hours needed at the present optimum solution. Below thirty-six hours the foundry capacity becomes critical and the shadow value of 0 does not hold. Thirty-six hours is therefore the *lower* limit of range for the shadow value of 0. In the case of the foundry, any increases in capacity have no effect and there is therefore no *upper* limit on the shadow value for the foundry constraint.

Consider increases in the capacity of the machine shop. (These, as we have seen, are equivalent to moving the constraint line outwards.) The upper limit of the range over which the shadow value on machine shop capacity will apply is reached when the new machine shop constraint line passes through the intersection of the foundry constraint line and the fitting bay constraint line (see point F in Figure 3.6). At this point $X_1 = 9.714$, $X_2 = 10.571$ and the machine shop hours required are:

$$3 \times 9.714 + 4 \times 10.571 = 71.43$$

It follows that the upper limit of the range over which the machine shop shadow value is applicable is 71·43 machine shop hours. The lower limit is reached when the new machine shop constraint line passes through point A in Figure 3.6. At this point $X_1 = 15$, $X_2 = 6$ and machine shop hours required are:

$$3 \times 15 + 4 \times 0 = 45$$

The lower limit of the range of applicability of the shadow value is therefore forty-five machine shop hours.

Similar arguments can be presented for the range over which the shadow value of the fitting bay constraint is applicable. Table 3.5 summarises all the results.

Sensitivity to profit coefficients

Another important question is: How does the optimum solution depend on cost or profit coefficient sensitivity? In the example being considered, profit is measured in terms of contribution to overheads. Suppose that the

Table 3.5

Ranges over which shadow values are applicable in Clarion Co. Ltd

Constraint	Capacity available (hours)	Shadow value of constraint	Capacity range over which the shadow value is applicable	
			Upper limit	Lower limit
Foundry	52	0	No limit	36
Machine shop	60	4·8	71·43	45
Fitting bay	60	8·4	80	40

coefficients in the objective function are of dubious accuracy. (After all cost and profit data often are inaccurate.) How might this affect the solution? For example the contribution to overheads from product 1 might drop from £48/unit to £36/unit. The objective function would then become:

$$Z = 36X_1 + 36X_2$$

The effect of this on the graph would be to rotate the lines of iso-profit slightly in an anticlockwise direction. However, it can be shown that the optimum solution would still be at point B. (Naturally the contribution to overheads would be affected because the contribution on product 1 has been reduced from £48 to £36/unit, but the optimum solution would still be at point B, i.e. where $X_1 = 12$ and $X_2 = 6$.)

A larger change in the contribution of X_1 is needed before the angle of the lines of iso-profit is altered sufficiently to change the optimum solution. The limiting value for contribution per unit of X_1 is the value at which the optimum solution moves from point B to point C. This could be arrived at by trial and error, i.e. drawing lines of iso-profit of decreasing inclination until one is found that just allows point C to be on a par with point B so far as profit is concerned. Looking at Figure 3.5, however, we can see that the limiting value must be the value at which the lines of iso-profit become parallel to the machine shop constraint line. If we keep the 36 figure for the contribution of X_2 constant, we see the limiting value will occur when the coefficients of the objective function are in the same ratio to one another as the coefficients in the machine shop constraint equation, i.e. when the contribution of X_2 is reduced to:

$$3 \times \frac{36}{4} = 27$$

In this case the objective function becomes:

$$Z = 27X_1 + 36X_2$$

The lower limiting value for the unit contribution of X_1 is therefore 27 £/unit if the solution to the problem is to remain unchanged. Below 27 £/unit the optimum solution moves from point B to point C. Suppose now that the unit contribution of X_1 increased above 48 £/unit. In this case the effect is to rotate the lines of iso-profit in a clockwise direction. The limiting value occurs when the unit contribution of X_1 increases from 48 £/unit to 72 £/unit, at which point the optimum solution moves from point B to point A. This means that above 72 £/unit contribution from X_1 it is optimal to produce only X_1 and none of X_2.

Similar unit contribution limits can be calculated as far as the second variable X_2 is concerned. (See Table 3.6.)

Table 3.6

Limiting ranges of contribution/unit product

Product	Contribution £/unit	Lower limit of contribution £/unit	Upper limit of contribution £/unit
X_1	48	27	72
X_2	36	24	64

Table 3.6 shows that the optimum solution was found for contribution values of £48 and £36 on the two products and this optimum solution is valid so long as the contribution figures stay within the limits £27–£72 in the case of product 1 and £24–£64 in the case of product 2. In this instance we have found that the optimum plan of making $X_1 = 12$ and $X_2 = 6$ is only affected by extreme changes in the contribution figures. Insensitivity of this sort is not unusual.

Contribution to overheads is, of course, only one way of measuring profitability. If we had formulated the problem in terms of profit as such, we would then have referred to a unit profit sensitivity analysis calculating the limiting ranges for the unit profit data. If the linear program had been formulated to minimise cost, a comparable exercise would be a cost sensitivity analysis and give limiting ranges for the cost/unit of each 'ingredient' in the solution.

In interpreting the results of a linear program, sensitivity analyses can be as valuable as the solution itself. We have seen the solution and sensitivity analyses in relation to a two-dimensional problem. These findings and their understanding are analogous to the kind of result obtained with more than two variables, although with more than two variables the results cannot be expressed graphically.

Conditions for the use of LP

Certain conditions must be satisfied before linear programming can be used. These are:

1 There must be a number of variables whose values are to be determined.

2 Negative values of the variables must be non-permissible.

3 All restrictions on the values of the variables must be expressible as linear inequalities in terms of the variables.

Thus:

$$\left.\begin{array}{l} 3X + 2Y \geqslant 8 \\ 2X + 9Y \leqslant 3 \\ X + Y = 4 \end{array}\right\} \quad \text{are allowable restrictions}$$

$$X^2 + Y^2 = 4 \quad \text{is not allowable}$$

where X and Y are the values of the variables; ($\leqslant$ means is less than or equal to; $\geqslant$ means is greater than or equal to).

4 There must be a single objective involving optimising a linear function of the variables.

5 The variables must be divisible to allow fractional amounts (although this condition can be lifted when the value of the variable is high; the solution: 'manufacture 489·7 gearboxes' could for example be interpreted as: 'manufacture 490 gearboxes' etc).

Introduction to formulating an LP

Formulation is the process of taking a problem situation and describing it in terms of equations. This was not difficult in the case of Clarion Co. Ltd, but in practice there can be considerable art attached to the formulation of a suitable linear program to solve a large scale practical problem. Often the same problem may be formulated in a number of different ways and the way in which it is formulated can affect the nature of the information that can be readily extracted from the results, as well as influencing the computer time and costs involved in reaching a solution. The following provides a simple example to introduce the fundamental steps in formulating a linear program.

The Drexel Company manufactures five products A, B, C, D and E. Each product requires the facilities of four departments in the company. Table 3.7 shows the machine times used in the four departments per unit manufactured, for each of the products. The right hand column shows the capacity available in the four departments in machine hours, and the bottom row of the table shows the unit profit which results from the manufacture of each product.

Table 3.7

Hours required in different departments to manufacture products at the Drexel Company

| | Machine hours required/unit of product | | | | | Capacity |
	A	B	C	D	E	(machine hours)
Department 1	2·0	4·2	4·0	3·0	4·2	12,000
Department 2	3·0	2·0	1·8	1·1	1·4	8,000
Department 3	2·0	4·0	1·6	2·0	1·1	14,000
Department 4	2·0	1·4	0·9	1·5	4·0	9,000
Profit £/unit of product	1·6	1·8	1·7	1·4	2·0	

The company already has firm commitments to supply 1,000 units of product B and 1,200 of product D. Given these prior commitments and the resources available, the company is interested in determining its optimum product mix to maximise profit. In other words, the company wants to know the best amounts of each product to produce to achieve maximum profit within the restrictions of its prior commitments and the resources available.

The first step in formulating the problem as an LP is to identify the variables. These are simply the quantities in the problem which are to be determined by the company.

In this case we want to know how many of each product we should make and therefore we simply say that the variables are:

X_1 = number of units of product A to be manufactured
X_2 = number of units of product B to be manufactured
X_3 = number of units of product C to be manufactured
X_4 = number of units of product D to be manufactured
X_5 = number of units of product E to be manufactured

The next step is to take account of the restrictions and limitations imposed in the problem. The first of these restrictions are those imposed by the limitations on available capacity in the various departments. Looking at Table 3.7 we can express the number of machine hours used in department 1 as:

$$2 \cdot 0 X_1 + 4 \cdot 2 X_2 + 4 \cdot 0 X_3 + 3 \cdot 0 X_4 + 4 \cdot 2 X_5$$

We also know that there are only 12,000 hours available in department 1. Therefore, since the machine hours to be used obviously cannot exceed the hours available, we write:
(Department 1)

$$2 \cdot 0 X_1 + 4 \cdot 2 X_2 + 4 \cdot 0 X_3 + 3 \cdot 0 X_4 + 4 \cdot 2 X_5 \leqslant 12{,}000$$

This is called a 'capacity constraint'.

The constraints imposed by limitations on manufacturing capacity in departments 2, 3 and 4 can be written similarly from the information in Table 3.7 as follows:
(Department 2)

$$3 \cdot 0 X_1 + 2 \cdot 0 X_2 + 1 \cdot 8 X_3 + 1 \cdot 1 X_4 + 1 \cdot 4 X_5 \leqslant 8{,}000$$

(Department 3)

$$2 \cdot 0 X_1 + 4 \cdot 0 X_2 + 1 \cdot 6 X_3 + 2 \cdot 0 X_4 + 1 \cdot 1 X_5 \leqslant 14{,}000$$

(Department 4)

$$2 \cdot 0 X_1 + 1 \cdot 4 X_2 + 0 \cdot 9 X_3 + 1 \cdot 5 X_4 + 4 \cdot 0 X_5 \leqslant 9{,}000$$

Note that we are not required to use all the capacity available in each department. All that is required is that the available capacities in the departments should not be exceeded. There are other conditions to be imposed relating to the commitments to supply at least 1,000 units of product B and 1,200 units of product D. We write these requirements as:

$$X_2 \geqslant 1{,}000$$

and

$$X_4 \geqslant 1{,}200$$

We have now formulated all the conditions of the problem. The next step is to look at the objective function.

Referring again to Table 3.7 the total profit can be written as:

$$Z = 1 \cdot 6 X_1 + 1 \cdot 8 X_2 + 1 \cdot 7 X_3 + 1 \cdot 4 X_4 + 2 \cdot 0 X_5$$

This equation is called the objective function.

Negative values of the variables are not allowed (we cannot plan to produce negative amounts). Therefore:

$$
\left.\begin{array}{l}
X_1 \geqslant 0 \\
X_2 \geqslant 0 \\
X_3 \geqslant 0 \\
X_4 \geqslant 0 \\
X_5 \geqslant 0
\end{array}\right\}
$$

We have now completed the formulation of the problem by converting it from a verbal description of the situation to a mathematical form consisting of variables, constraint equations and an objective function. It is now necessary to find the values of the variables X_1, X_2, X_3, X_4 and X_5 which maximise the objective function subject to the conditions of the constraint equations and with the condition that non-negative values of the variables are not permitted.

A procedure for solving this problem by systematically trying different possibilities is called the Simplex procedure. It leads to the optimum solution shown in Table 3.8.

Table 3.8

Optimum solution for the Drexel Company product mix problem

Variable	Value	Profit/unit	Profit on product line
X_1	1,405·71	1·6	2,249·14
X_2	1,000·00	1·8	1,800·00
X_4	1,200·00	1·4	1,680·00
X_5	330·61	2·0	661·22
		Total profit	6,390·36

We can infer, since X_3 is not mentioned in the solution, that no units of product C are to be produced. We obviously cannot produce fractional units as indicated by the computer solution, but an adequately accurate answer will be obtained if we round off the figures to:

$$
\begin{array}{l}
X_1 = 1,406 \\
X_2 = 1,000 \\
X_4 = 1,200 \\
X_5 = 331
\end{array}
$$

(This still produces a total profit of approximately £6,390.)

The steps which we have carried out in formulating this problem are common to all linear programming applications and can be summarised by recalling the three main features of a linear programming problem, namely:

1 *Variables*   : Identify the variables in the problem.
2 *Constraints*   : Write down the appropriate constraint equations, in terms of the variables.
3 *Objective function* : Select a suitable objective function which is expressed in terms of the variables.

Slack variables

In order to interpret the results from the Simplex algorithm it is helpful to have some knowledge of how the method works.

Consider the following LP.

Maximise:
$$Z = 0.6X_1 + 0.7X_2 + 0.5X_3$$
subject to:
$$2.4X_1 + 3.0X_2 + 2.0X_3 \leqslant 1{,}200$$
$$0X_1 + 2.5X_2 + 1.5X_3 \leqslant 600$$
$$5X_1 + 0X_2 + 2.5X_3 \leqslant 1{,}500$$

and X_1, X_2, X_3 non-negative.

The first stage in the Simplex procedure is to introduce three new variables (known as *slack* variables):

$X_4 =$ the extent to which the LHS is less than the RHS in the first constraint

$X_5 =$ the extent to which the LHS is less than the RHS in the second constraint

$X_6 =$ the extent to which the LHS is less than the RHS in the third constraint.

We then have:

$$2.4X_1 + 3.0X_2 + 2.0X_3 + X_4 = 1{,}200$$
$$0X_1 + 2.5X_2 + 1.5X_3 + X_5 = 600$$
$$5X_1 + 0X_2 + 2.5X_3 + X_6 = 1{,}500$$
$$X_1, X_2, X_3 \text{ positive}$$
$$\text{and} \quad X_4, X_5, X_6 \text{ positive}$$

The '$\leqslant$' constraints in the original formulation have been converted into '$=$' constraints in the new formulation by the introduction of the three slack variables X_4, X_5 and X_6. The original variables in the problem (X_1, X_2 and X_3) are known as *structural* variables. Slack and structural variables need not be regarded as markedly different. They must both be non-negative in value. The objective function can be written:

Maximise: $0.6X_1 + 0.7X_2 + 0.5X_3 + 0X_4 + 0X_5 + 0X_6$

We will compare the more general situation with the two-dimensional case. In the two-dimensional case it was demonstrated that the solution must be either (a) at the intersection of two constraint lines, or (b) at the intersection of a constraint line and one of the axes.

Now, on a constraint line, the corresponding slack variables must be zero. Hence (a) corresponds to two slack variables being zero and (b) corresponds to one slack and one structural variable being zero. In either (a) or (b) two of the total number of variables are zero. Thus the total number of non-zero variables (structural and slacks) in the optimum solution is equal to the number of constraints. This provides an illustration of the general rule:

The number of variables (slack and structural) which are non-zero in an optimum LP solution is never greater than the number of constraints. Optimum solutions where the number of non-zero variables is actually less than the number of constraints are called degenerate and are very rare. In general, therefore, *the number of non-zero variables must equal the number of constraints.*

Returning to the example above:

maximise: $0.6X_1 + 0.7X_2 + 0.5X_3 + 0X_4 + 0X_5 + 0X_6$

subject to:
$$2.4X_1 + 3.0X_2 + 2.0X_3 + X_4 \qquad\qquad = 1{,}200$$
$$0X_1 + 2.5X_2 + 1.5X_3 + X_5 \qquad\quad = 600$$
$$5X_1 + 0X_2 + 2.5X_3 + X_6 = 1{,}500$$

We are interested in all solutions to the three equations which have at most three non-zero variables. One of these will we know be the optimum solution (i.e. it will maximise the objective function).

At this stage it is appropriate to introduce some terminology. Suppose there are m constraints.

A basic feasible solution is a solution satisfying the constraint equations which is such that there are at most m non-zero variables. The non-zero variables in a basic feasible solution are called *basic variables* and are said to form a *basis*. The variables which are zero are called *non-basic variables*.

The Simplex algorithm is simply a systematic procedure for testing basic feasible solutions to see which one is optimal. In this case it starts with what might be termed the 'obvious' solution, which puts all the slack variables into the basis. In the case of the above example this obvious solution is:

$$X_1 = 0 \quad X_4 = 1,200$$
$$X_2 = 0 \quad X_5 = \quad 600$$
$$X_3 = 0 \quad X_6 = 1,500$$

It then tests systematically whether the profit can be improved by replacing one of the basic variables by a non-basic variable. If the profit can be improved it brings into the basis that variable which will improve profit most, removing from the basis another variable at the same time. In the above example it would eventually reach the optimal solution.

$$X_1 = 180$$
$$X_2 = \quad 96 \quad X_4, X_5, X_6 = 0$$
$$X_3 = 240$$

(Note, incidentally, that it is *not* always the case that no slack variables are left in the optimal solution.)

In many problems the solution method will also have to deal with constraints of the ' $\geqslant$ ' type, for example:

$$3X_1 + 2X_2 + X_3 \geqslant 400$$

The ' $\geqslant$ ' type constraint is converted into an ' $=$ ' constraint by *subtracting* a slack variable:

$X_7 =$ the extent to which the LHS is greater than the RHS of the above constraint.

Then:

$$3X_1 + 2X_2 + X_3 - X_7 = 400$$

In the case of ' $=$ ' type constraints there is of course no need to introduce a slack variable. Constraints of the ' $\geqslant$ ' and ' $=$ ' type pose slightly more difficulty in establishing an initial feasible solution than the simple case with only ' $\leqslant$ ' type constraints illustrated above. There are a number of satisfactory techniques for finding an initial basic feasible solution when there are a mixture of ' $\leqslant$ ', ' $\geqslant$ ' and ' $=$ ' constraints. The solution is then improved in the way already described until an optimum solution is reached.

The output from an LP

Computer programs are available for the solution of LP problems. Usually these programs will automatically insert the appropriate slack variables for the user. The solution then supplies information as to which of the constraints, if any, have slack in the optimum solution and the amount of that slack. In addition to the optimum solution most computer procedures provide a sensitivity analysis for values of the profit/cost coefficients in the objective function and the shadow values of the constraints. This is illustrated in the following example.

Example: The Laurence Valley Rock Crushing Co. Ltd

A hydroelectric project involves building a road in the Laurence Valley. It requires 10,000 tonnes of crushed rock to the following specification:

Not more than 10 per cent dust
At least 34 per cent fine gravel
At least 30 per cent medium rocks
Not more than 20 per cent large rocks

Rock can be obtained locally from the head of the Laurence Valley or brought in from nearby Allerton. The rock crusher can be operated at two settings, either 'fine operation' or 'normal operation'. The proportions of dust, fine gravel, medium rocks and large rocks in the output depend on the setting of the crusher, and whether the rock is from the Laurence Valley or Allerton. The proportions and costs are shown in Table 3.9.

Table 3.9
Output from crusher in rock crushing example

	Fine operation		Normal operation	
	Allerton rock (%)	Laurence rock (%)	Allerton rock (%)	Laurence rock (%)
Dust	14	15	3	6
Fine gravel	46	45	20	24
Medium rocks	30	25	49	40
Large rocks	10	15	28	30
Cost fr./tonne	16·8	3·2	16·1	2·5

Cost figures are costs in francs/tonne of output and take into account the cost of the rock, transport and electricity to drive the crusher.

There are only 6,000 tonnes of local Laurence rock available to be put through the crusher.

There is another source of possible material: some ready crushed rock, 1,500 tonnes in all, left over from a previous exercise, has the following specification.

40

Dust 10 per cent
Fine gravel 25 per cent
Medium rocks 28 per cent
Large rocks 37 per cent

Head Office believe that this ready crushed rock should be used first. Define the variables in this problem as:

X_1 = amount of Allerton rock crushed–fine operation–tonnes
X_2 = amount of Laurence rock crushed–fine operation–tonnes
X_3 = amount of Allerton rock crushed–medium operation–tonnes
X_4 = amount of Laurence rock crushed–medium operation–tonnes
X_5 = amount of existing crushed rock employed–tonnes.

The results of crushing X_1, X_2, X_3, X_4, X_5, added together have to meet the required specification for 10,000 tonnes. This imposes the following constraints:

$$0.14X_1 + 0.15X_2 + 0.03X_3 + 0.06X_4$$
$$+ 0.1X_5 \leqslant 1{,}000 \text{ (maximum dust–tonnes)}$$
$$0.46X_1 + 0.45X_2 + 0.20X_3 + 0.24X_4$$
$$+ 0.25X_5 \geqslant 3{,}400 \text{ (minimum gravel–tonnes)}$$
$$0.30X_1 + 0.25X_2 + 0.49X_3 + 0.40X_4$$
$$+ 0.28X_5 \geqslant 3{,}000 \text{ (minimum medium rocks–tonnes)}$$
$$0.10X_1 + 0.15X_2 + 0.28X_3 + 0.30X_4$$
$$+ 0.37X_5 \leqslant 2{,}000 \text{ (maximum large rocks–tonnes)}$$
$$X_1 + X_2 + X_3 + X_4 + X_5 = 10{,}000 \text{ (total quantity–tonnes)}$$

There are only 6,000 tonnes of Laurence rock available, therefore:

$$X_2 + X_4 \leqslant 6{,}000$$

and only 1,500 tonnes of existing crushed rock, therefore:

$$X_5 \leqslant 1{,}500$$

The objective is to minimise cost. The cost, if any, of using the existing crushed rock is not mentioned in the problem. As a trial solution it is reasonable to enter it as zero, giving the following cost function to be minimised:

Minimise: $Z = 16.8X_1 + 3.2X_2 + 16.1X_3 + 2.5X_4 + 0X_5$

subject to the above constraints.

Data values for the number of variables, the number of constraints, the coefficients of the constraints, the coefficients of the cost function to be minimised, the right hand sides of the constraints and the nature of the constraints ($\leqslant$, $\geqslant$ or $=$) were fed into a suitable computer program. The optimum solution was produced in Table 3.10.

Table 3.10

Optimum solution to rock crushing example

Variable	Value	Cost/unit	Cost
X_1	684·9	16·8	11506·3
X_2	5205·5	3·2	16657·6
X_3	4109·6	16·1	66164·6
		Total cost	94328·5

Table 3.10 tells us that, given the formulation of the problem, the most economical solution is to use 684·9 tonnes of X_1, 5205·5 tonnes of X_2 and 4109·6 tonnes of X_3. The total cost is 94328·5 fr., i.e. 9·4 fr./tonne. The cost/unit column provides a note of the cost coefficients which were input. The right hand cost column shows how the total cost is made up from costs incurred on the various activities X_1, X_2 and X_3. Note that the minimum cost solution makes no use of the ready crushed rock X_5, even though it was entered at zero cost.

A sensitivity analysis on the cost coefficients gives more information (see Tables 3.11 and 3.12).

Table 3.11

Sensitivity analysis on cost coefficients for basic variables

Variable	Cost/unit	Cost range	
		Upper limit	Lower limit
X_1	16·8	–	16·3
X_2	3·2	3·62	–
X_3	16·1	16·63	−32·16

Table 3.12

Sensitivity analysis on cost coefficients for non-basic variable

Variable	Cost/unit	Penalty rate	Lower limit
X_4	2·5	0·43	2·07
X_5	0·0	25·57	−25·57

Table 3.11 shows the sensitivity of the solution to the basic (non-zero) variables. The lower limit of the X_1 cost coefficient is 16·3. This means that, provided the unit cost of X_1 is not below 16·3, the stated solution is still optimal (all other variables being assumed to remain fixed). In this case the solution is therefore quite sensitive to changes in the unit cost of X_1. If the unit cost of X_1 was for some reason below 16·3, the program would have to be re-run to find the new optimum solution. On the other hand there is no upper limit shown for the unit cost of X_1. If the unit cost of X_1 is increased by any amount the given optimal solution is still optimal. The implication is that the stated requirements of the problem cannot be met without using that amount of X_1. (If X_1 did increase excessively in cost one would of course look for an alternative source of suitable material. This would involve bringing an additional variable into the formulation to represent the alternative source and re-running the program. Alternatively if the cost was inordinate one could consider changing the requirements.) The reverse situation applies in the case of X_2, which yields a higher content of dust and large rocks (both undesirable). The upper limit for the unit cost of X_2 is shown as 3·62. This means that the given solution is still optimal if the cost of X_2 is above the data figure of 3·2 fr./tonne but not more than 3·62 fr./tonne. (If the cost of X_2 were above 3·62 fr./tonne, the computer program should be re-run with the new unit cost figure to obtain a new optimum solution.) No lower limit is shown for X_2. This implies that there is no way of exploiting a cost reduction in X_2 while still meeting the specification. Note that the lower limit of unit cost of X_3 is shown as negative, $-32·16$. This means that X_3 would have to be available at zero cost with a subsidy of 32·16 fr./tonne before one should consider a different optimal solution.

Table 3.12 shows the sensitivity to unit cost of the non-basic variables. In the case of X_4 the lower limit is 2·07 fr./tonne. Therefore if the unit cost of X_4 dropped below 2·07, one should re-run the computer program to obtain the new optimal solution. X_5 is of special interest, as it represents the ready crushed rock which Head Office would like to see used first. The penalty rate of 25·57 fr./tonne means that if, in spite of what the optimal solution says, one insisted on using the ready crushed rock, the total cost would increase by 25·57 francs per tonne of ready crushed rock used. For example, if 120 tonnes of the ready crushed rock were used, the penalty rate shows the total cost (fr.) would increase to:

$$94328·5 + 120 \times 25·57 = 97396·9$$

The reason for this is that the ready crushed rock has a high proportion of large rocks and would require a greater proportion of the expensive X_1

with lesser amounts of the cheaper X_2 to stay within the specification. This can be confirmed by carrying out trial calculations with the original problem data. Thus the penalty rate gives a warning of cost implications in using a variable which has not been included in the optimum solution.

A report of the amounts of slack and the shadow values of the slack variables is shown in Table 3.13.

Table 3.13

Analysis of constraints for rock crushing example

Constraint	Type	Specified amount	Slack	Shadow value	Ranges	
Max. dust	$\leqslant$	1,000	0	330·6	948	– 1,032
Min. gravel	$\geqslant$	3,400	79·5	0	$-\infty$	– 3,479·5
Min. med.	$\geqslant$	3,000	520·5	0	$-\infty$	– 3,520·5
Max. large	$\leqslant$	2,000	0	205·9	1,654·5	– 2,041·7
Total quantity	$=$	10,000	0	83·7	9,866·7	–11,049·7
Available at Laurence	$\leqslant$	6,000	794·5	0	$-\infty$	– 5,205·5
Existing crushed rock	$\leqslant$	1,500	1,500	0	$-\infty$	– $+\infty$

We can see at once that the limiting constraints are 'max. dust' and 'max. large rocks' (and of course the total quantity, which is an equality constraint). Varying amounts of slack are shown on the other constraints. The shadow value of 330·6 fr./tonne for the max. dust constraint means that the total cost would be reduced by 330·6 francs for each tonne by which the max. dust of 1,000 tonnes could be relaxed. Alternatively it is the cost increase if the max. dust condition were tightened. For example, if the 1,000 tonnes dust condition were relaxed to 1,007 tonnes the overall cost would be reduced by: $7 \times 330 \cdot 6 = 2314 \cdot 2$ fr. The range 1032–948 means that this rate of cost decrease/increase for relaxation/tightening of the 1,000 tonnes dust constraint applies within that range. Outside the range, new variables would enter the basis and the optimum solution would have to be re-calculated. There is the possibility that outside the stated range, e.g. below 948, a feasible solution might be unobtainable.

The shadow value for the min. gravel constraint is zero. This is because there is slack on that constraint, and therefore a relaxation or a small tightening of the constraint has no effect. (It must always be the case that

44

the shadow value of a constraint on which there is slack is zero.) Note that the upper limit of the range for zero shadow value of the 'max. dust' constraint is 3479·5. This corresponds to the situation where all the slack is used up.

LP in practice

Realistic LP problems are almost invariably of a size and complexity which require the use of a computer. Most computer manufacturers and time-sharing bureaux provide LP computer packages. These are of varying degrees of complexity and range from packages capable of handling hundreds of variables and constraints to the small time-sharing procedures capable of handling forty or fifty variables and about the same number of constraints.

When LP is used in a routine fashion on a particular type of problem it is very useful to have a system which will automatically generate the LP formulation from the basic problem data. The procedures used to set up such a system are called 'Matrix Generators' and are available with the more advanced LP packages. They are usually used in conjunction with 'Report Writers' which are computer procedures designed to present the results in the terms of the problem rather than in the more general terms of LP.

The use of LP is based on the assumption that the constraints and the objective function are linear. This assumption is often an adequate approximation for practical purposes. It is worth noting, however, that there are special techniques for dealing with non-linearities in the more general field of mathematical programming – but at the cost of increased complexity and increased computer time. Linear programming also assumes infinite divisibility in the variables. This is not a problem if the values are fairly large and can be satisfactorily rounded to the nearest whole number. Where the values are small and the number of possible combinations to be considered in rounding off is large, the problem can be resolved using integer programming – again at the expense of a considerable increase in computer time.

One area where the application of LP has been particularly successful has been in the oil industry. In a number of companies, LP is used on a routine basis to determine the allocation of crude oils to the refineries and the operating schedules necessary at the refineries to produce the required mix of final products at minimum cost. A non-industrial application of LP is in the area of agricultural planning. Constraints include the availability of land and labour, capital limitations and requirements for crop rotation. LP is used to determine the most economic mix of farming activities given the available resources. More detailed descriptions of these and other applications of LP are given in the references at the end of this chapter.

LP has most commonly been used for the solution of tactical problems like material blending or production scheduling. It is now being used by many organisations to assist in strategic planning. Once an LP model has been constructed it can be used to determine the effects of various strategies and assumptions. Sometimes LP and simulation are used together. LP is used to obtain a solution to a problem in aggregate terms. Simulation is then used to explore the implications of the solution in more detail.

References

Further reading

Driebeek, N.J., *Applied Linear Programming,* Addison-Wesley, 1969.

Gass, S.I., *Linear Programming, Methods and Applications,* McGraw-Hill, 1958.

Hadley, G., *Linear Programming,* Addison-Wesley, 1962.

Haley, K.B., *Mathematical Programming in Business and Industry,* Macmillan, 1967.

Smith, D., *Linear Programming Models in Business,* Polytech, 1973.

Williams, N., *Linear and Non-Linear Programming in Industry,* Pitman, 1967.

Vajda, S., *Mathematical Programming,* Addison-Wesley, 1961.

Applications

Aronofsky, J.S. and Williams, A.C., 'The Use of Linear Programming in Oil Production', *Management Science,* vol. 8, no. 4, 1962, p. 394.

Beale, E.M.L., *Mathematical Programming in Practice,* Pitman, 1968.

Beale, E.M.L., 'A Management Advisory Service Using Computerised Optimisation Techniques', *Outlook on Agriculture,* vol. 6, no. 4, 1970.

Chappell, A.E., 'Linear Programming Cuts Costs in Production of Animal Feeds', *Operational Research Quarterly,* vol. 25, no. 1, 1975.

Fabian, T., 'Application of Linear Programming to Steel Production Planning', *J. Opns. Res. Soc. Am.,* vol. 3, no. 4, 1955, p. 565.

Salkin, G. and Kornbluth, J., *Linear Programming in Financial Planning,* Haymarket, 1973.

Smith, B., 'Planning Transistor Production by Linear Programming', *Operations Research,* vol. 13, no. 1, 1965, p. 132.

Exercises

1 A factory produces two grades of thermal/acoustic insulating board, called red band and blue band, for private dwellings.

The machinery used to process this board has capacity for a total output of 3,000 sq. ft. per day total of red and blue band board. Both types of board use two process chemicals which are in limited supply. Red band board requires 0·5 litres of process chemical I per sq. ft. of board and 0·525 litres of process chemical II per sq. ft. of board. Each sq. ft. of blue band board manufactured requires 0·3 litres of process chemical I and 0·75 litres of process chemical II. These two chemicals are available in the following quantities:

Chemical I : 1,200 litres per day

Chemical II : 2,100 litres per day

Profits on the manufacture of the board are 1·8p per sq. ft. of red band board and 1·2p per sq. ft. of blue band board.

(1) Formulate the linear program and obtain the solution which maximises profit.

(2) Would the profit which can be obtained be affected by a firm commitment to supply a customer with 1,800 sq. ft. per day of blue band board, and, if so, by how much?

2 A manufacturer of electric motors has obsolescent material in his store as the result of a planned changeover to new products.

Special copper wire 10,000 lb.

Electrical sheet steel stampings 20,000 lb.

He also has 5,000 man-hours surplus labour capacity.

He can manufacture the materials into three different types of motor:

Type I requires

50 lb copper, 100 lb sheet steel and 100 man-hours.

Type II requires

50 lb copper, 80 lb sheet steel and 50 man-hours.

Type III requires

60 lb copper, 50 lb sheet steel and 10 man-hours.

The profit he can obtain per motor on each of these three types is:
  Type I   £10
  Type II   £20
  Type III £5
How many should he make of each motor so as to maximise profit from the obsolete material and surplus labour capacity? Formulate the linear program.

3   A company blends ingredients to produce animal feedstuffs. Possible ingredients for a poultry food mix are listed in the following table together with their nutritional properties and cost/ton.

Ingredient no.	Protein (%)	Calcium (%)	Phos. (%)	Metabolic energy cal/lb	Cost £/ton
1 Maize	9	0·02	0·27	1,555	135
2 Barley	10	0·06	0·37	1,420	120
3 Beans	27	0·12	0·4	1,100	65
4 Cotton seed	39	0·24	1·2	850	84
5 Groundnuts	50	0·16	0·55	1,000	130
6 Limestone flour	–	39	–	–	15

The nutritional requirements are:
  Protein $\geq$ 15 per cent
  Calcium $\geq$ 3·4 per cent
  Calcium $\leq$ 3·6 per cent
  Phosphorus $\geq$ 0·4 per cent
  Metabolic energy $\geq$ 1,220 cal/lb
Formulate the constraints and objective function to give a least cost food mix, meeting the nutritional requirements.

4   Marine Drive Ltd manufacture three sizes of forward/reverse clutch-gearboxes in sizes M600, M700 and M800.
  To make one M600 gearbox requires 10 hours fabrication, 150 hours machining and 60 hours fitting and assembly.
  The M700 size requires 50 hours fabrication, 240 hours machining and 50 hours fitting and assembly.
  The M800 size requires 100 hours fabrication, 300 hours machining and 50 hours fitting and assembly.

Manufacturing capacity of the concern is 10,000 hours per month fitting and assembly, 40,000 hours per month machining and 5,000 hours per month fabrication.

The whole of the output of Marine Drive Ltd is sold to Marine Propulsion Sales Ltd, at a profit to Marine Drive Ltd of £1,000 per M600 unit, £4,000 per M700 unit and £3,500 per M800 unit.

Formulate the linear program.

5 A company manufactures paper for electrical insulation in rolls of a standard width of 200 in. The paper is then slit from the standard width to suit customers' individual requirements. (The nominal length of paper on a roll is 1,000 ft.)

On a particular shift there are orders as follows:

Width	Number of rolls required
60 in	96
70 in	209
85 in	165
120 in	94

Formulate a linear program to meet the customer requirements, minimising the number of rolls to be cut. (The problem can be formulated as an LP by recognising that there are a number of reasonable ways in which the required widths might be slit from the stock width. The variables in the problem are the number of stock rolls to be slit to each of these patterns.)

6 A company has three bales of scrap in the melting shop. The composition of the bales and their weights are given in the following table.

Bale no.	Copper (%)	Zinc (%)	Tin (%)	Antimony (%)	Weight (lb)
1	71	22	6	1	600
2	60	36	4		400
3	84		14	2	300

The bales are taken at their scrap valuation of 18p/lb.

It is required to make up a new alloy as follows:

Copper	Max. 78 per cent	Min. 67 per cent
Zinc	Max. 18 per cent	Min. 12 per cent
Tin	Max. 8 per cent	
Antimony		Min. 1 per cent

The shop has unlimited supplies of pure copper, zinc and tin at the following costs:

Copper	32p/lb
Zinc	21p/lb
Tin	163p/lb
Antimony	406p/lb

Formulate an LP to determine a suitable blend of amounts from the scrap bales and pure metals to produce 1,000 lb of the new alloy at minimum cost.

Case B HIBAL Aluminium

HIBAL Aluminium have recently set up an Operations Analysis and Planning Unit. Alan Thompson, the head of the unit, has several years' experience with HIBAL and a special interest in the application of model building techniques in management. The Operations Analysis and Planning Unit has access to the company's computer, and uses a time-sharing service for the evaluation of smaller scale models.

Background and company operations

The raw material of aluminium is bauxite (hydrated aluminium oxide ore). This is first concentrated and purified in a refining plant to yield alumina (aluminium oxide). The bauxite ore is relatively impure, and as much as seventeen tons of bauxite can be required to produce one ton of alumina. The alumina is smelted by electrolytic action to produce aluminium ingots. The smelting process requires large quantities of electricity, and for this reason it is usual to locate the smelters close to sources of relatively cheap electric power.

HIBAL sell aluminium ingots in both the UK and the South of France. The company was formed in 1958, by combining UK interests in aluminium production and distribution on the eastern seaboard of Canada with an aluminium production and sales company based at Bezier on the Mediterranean coast of France. The combined company was originally formed to serve markets in Canada, the UK and the South of France. HIBAL has long-standing arrangements for the supply of ore from Kingston (Jamaica) and Boké (Guinea). Three years ago HIBAL completed construction of a new smelter at Peterhead (Scotland) with capacity to supply 2,500 tons of ingots per week, primarily to the UK market. This plant has seldom been able to run at full capacity, mainly due to labour difficulties, and last year capacity was reduced by 20 per cent due to shortfalls in the electricity supply. The smelter at Bezier has a capacity of 3,000 tons of ingots per week. HIBAL recently sold its smelting and distribution business on the east coast of Canada because of fierce competition from Canadian aluminium producers, and in anticipation of a slump in the Canadian market. The company has retained a small refining plant at Halifax (Nova Scotia) with a capacity to handle 25,000 tons of bauxite per week. HIBAL also operates a refining plant at Old Harbour Bay (Jamaica) with capacity to handle 45,000 tons of bauxite per week and a new 45,000 tons per week refining plant at Peterhead. Exhibit 1 shows the international nature of HIBAL's operations.

The Boké mine, which is now locally owned and operated, supplies bauxite ore to HIBAL under an agreement limiting the amounts supplied to not more than 55,000 tons per week at a price of £4·1 a ton. The bauxite ore supplied from Boké has a 5·9 per cent yield by weight of alumina. The Boké mine operators would be prepared to supply ore of this quality in excess of 55,000 tons per week, but at a re-negotiated price which would probably be in the region of £6 a ton for the excess amounts. The Kingston mine is still owned and operated by HIBAL and has a mining capacity of 60,000 tons of bauxite per week at a cost of £6·5 a ton. The Kingston ore is of higher quality giving a yield of 10·5 per cent by weight of alumina.

The cost of refining bauxite ore to alumina varies slightly between the three plants, being £3·5 a ton of alumina at Old Harbour Bay, £4·2 a ton at Halifax and £4·8 a ton at the new plant in Peterhead. The company has nearly always been short of refined alumina to feed its smelters. Two years ago, when alumina demand was at a record level, HIBAL bought in large quantities of refined alumina from Greece in order to do everything possible to meet its customers' demand for HIBAL ingots. Alan noted that, if they were still buying in alumina from Greece, the current price would be about £180 a ton delivered at Bezier.

Current smelting costs are £88 a ton of aluminium smelted at Bezier and £74 a ton at Peterhead. The Bezier plant gives a yield of 41 per cent by weight of aluminium from alumina. At the Peterhead plant the corresponding yield is 43 per cent.

Market trends and forecasts

Demand for HIBAL aluminium had started to fall back in both France and the UK some eighteen months ago. By the end of the first six periods of the year just completed demand had fallen to 20 per cent below the year's earlier level. On the basis of current economic trends it is believed that demand has now bottomed out. The current selling price for HIBAL ingots is £510 a ton. In the longer term demand should begin to increase by the end of the second quarter of the current year, with the possibility of a rapid return to conditions where demand for HIBAL aluminium in France and the UK exceeds supply.

HIBAL demand forecasts are revised every four weeks. Exhibit 2 shows the comparison between forecasts and actual demand for the year just completed, and the forecast for the first period of the new year.

Assignment

Alan Thompson's job is to make recommendations as to the overall operating levels in the various parts of the company, for the next period, and consider the possible implications for the future. (A note on transportation costs is given in Exhibit 3, and Exhibit 4 shows the interrelationship between the various operating units.)

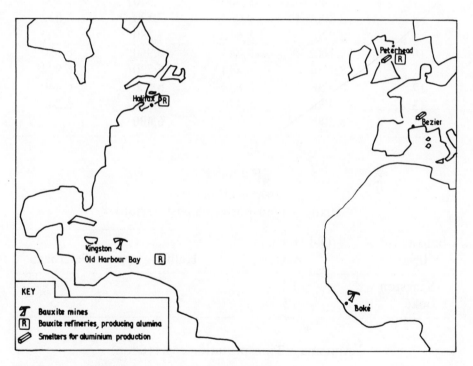

Exhibit 1   HIBAL international operations

Exhibit 2
HIBAL aluminium demand (tons)
Forecast versus actuals (4 weekly periods)

Period number	France		UK	
	Forecast	Actual	Forecast	Actual
1	10,840	10,404	7,800	8,284
2	10,400	10,920	8,000	7,768
3	10,280	9,968	7,920	7,740
4	10,000	9,000	7,760	7,848
5	10,040	10,240	7,560	7,388
6	9,680	10,744	7,440	6,920
7	9,240	8,960	7,320	7,804
8	8,800	9,064	7,520	8,032
9	8,820	8,640	7,280	7,000
10	9,160	8,884	6,960	6,680
11	8,720	8,444	6,720	6,924
12	8,720	8,828	6,600	6,440
13	8,400	8,440	6,160	6,240
1	8,200	–	6,400	–

Exhibit 3
Transportation costs
Bauxite – Transportation costs (£/ton)

Bauxite to → from ↓	Old Harbour Bay	Halifax	Peterhead
Kingston	0·2	3·2	7·1
Boké	6·5	5·9	5·5

Alumina – Transportation costs (£/ton)

Alumina to → from ↓	Bezier	Peterhead
Old Harbour Bay	7·9	8·5
Halifax	5·6	5·3
Peterhead	3·5	0·1

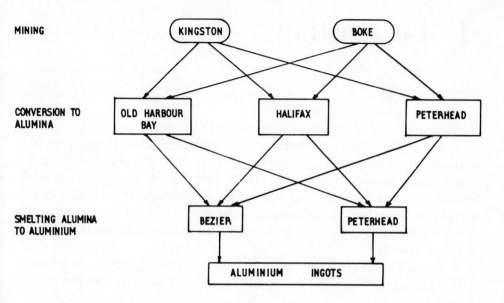

MINING

CONVERSION TO
ALUMINA

SMELTING ALUMINA
TO ALUMINIUM

Exhibit 4   Bauxite to aluminium conversion

4 Forecasting

An important use of quantitative models is in the prediction of the future. In order to plan and control effectively, management needs estimates of future levels of sales, costs, manpower requirements, raw material requirements and a variety of other factors. In fact, before taking almost any decision, a manager must make a number of forecasts about future conditions and the effects of various courses of action. These forecasts may be made only mentally, even subconsciously, but they are a necessary part of decision making.

When forecasts have to be made on the basis of past data, a manager has two main approaches available to him, (a) using intuition, and (b) using a model.

The use of intuition involves experience, knowledge of the market, flair etc., and its importance should not be underestimated. However, when used alone, it does have a number of drawbacks.

1   Intuitive forecasts tend to be biased. This is partly due to the personality of the forecaster and whether he is an optimist or a pessimist, but also to confusion between targets and forecasts. If the forecast is to be used as a target, individuals will set forecasts on the low side. On the other hand, if the forecast is to be used as a basis for budget allocations, individuals will set forecasts on the high side to increase their share of the total budget.
2   It is difficult to forecast the limits of accuracy for an intuitive forecast.
3   The time of people with the skill and knowledge to make such forecasts is expensive.
4   In many forecasting situations, for example, stock control, a very large number of separate forecasts have to be made and the use of intuitive forecasting can be very time-consuming.

Model building is a way of overcoming these drawbacks. If the model is chosen correctly there will be no bias. Furthermore, the error in a forecast can be estimated and, generally, if a large number of forecasts are required, they can be produced in a routine way by either a junior clerk or a computer at relatively low cost. However, a forecast which is produced by model building is sometimes no more than an extrapolation of past data. It may ignore the effects of changes in government policy, increases in the number of competitors and any other events which are not reflected in the past data.

The basic methodology

This chapter is primarily concerned with the way in which model building can be used in short term forecasting (i.e. in situations where a forecast is being produced two to three months in advance). Whatever the model being used, the basic procedure is always the same.

1   *Analyse past data.* When data has been collected together for the past few years, it should be possible to distinguish several different sources of variation.

> (a)   Trend effect – a steady increase or decrease with time. In the short term we can assume the trend is linear.
> (b)   Seasonal variation – a cyclic pattern which is repeated over each twelve month period.
> (c)   Random variation – additional variation which cannot be explained by the trend or the seasonal pattern.
> Random and seasonal variation should be removed from the figures so that the trend can be estimated. The seasonally adjusted figures should be compared with the actual figures so that the seasonal effect for each time period can be calculated.

2   *Prepare the forecast.* The deseasonalised figures should be extrapolated into the future and the appropriate value of the seasonal effect should then be incorporated.

3   *Calculate forecasting error.* Each forecast should be compared with the actual result to give a measure of forecasting error. If the forecasting accuracy is insufficient for the intended purpose, then an improved method of forecasting must be devised. Even when a forecasting method is known to be capable of giving the required accuracy, the forecasting error should still be monitored. Any sudden change in conditions, for example a dramatic change in the trend, will be quickly revealed by the increase in forecasting error and appropriate action can be taken.

4   *Incorporate additional factors.* The forecast produced assumes that the existing pattern of data will continue in the future. The forecast may need altering to allow for large changes which have not been allowed for in the forecasting model. Examples of such changes are:

> (a)   a major change in company policy, as might occur after a merger;

(b) a major change in competitive policy, for example when a powerful new competitor emerges;

(c) a major change in government policy.

5 *Apply the forecast.* The forecast is merely an aid to management decision making. If the forecast predicts an unsatisfactory state of affairs, then immediate action should be taken to ensure that the forecast is not fulfilled.

Moving averages

The simplest approach to forecasting using past data is to assume that in the short run the underlying mean is constant with the actual data being subject to random fluctuations about the mean (see Figure 4.1). We might choose to average the previous six values in an attempt to estimate this underlying mean and use it as our forecast. This procedure is called the moving average method.

The length of time over which a moving average is taken will vary according to choice and circumstances, and three month and twelve month moving averages are all relatively common. The method by which a moving average can be calculated is shown in Table 4.1.

Table 4.1

Calculation of moving averages

Month (1)	Demand (2)	Total demand in last 6 months (3)	6 month moving average (4)	Forecast (5)
1	31			
2	29			
3	30			
4	33			
5	34			
6	29	186	31	
7				31

Suppose that it is now the end of month 6.

The total of the previous six months' demands is:

$$31 + 29 + 30 + 33 + 34 + 29 = 186$$

as shown in column 3.

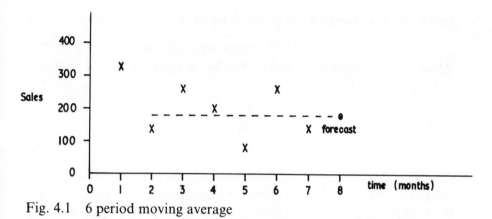

Fig. 4.1   6 period moving average

The 6 month average is: $186/6 = 31$, as shown in column 4.

Note that we use the moving average as the forecast of the next demand in month 7, as shown in column 5 of the table. When we know the demand in month 7, the moving average is updated to forecast month 8.

Suppose the actual demand in month 7 is thirty-seven units. We could update the 6 month moving average by re-calculating for what, after month 7, would be the previous six months, i.e. months 2, 3, 4, 5, 6 and 7, and proceed as before. This would be correct, but there is an easier way. The previous total was 186. If we subtract from this the earliest demand which occurred in that total and add the latest demand we have:

$$\text{New total} = 186 - 31 + 37$$
$$= 186 + 6 = 192$$

This gives the same result as adding the demand figures for months 2, 3, 4, 5, 6 and 7.

The new moving average is $192/6 = 32$.

Continuing the table:

Month	Demand	Total demand in last 6 months	6 month moving average	Forecast
7	37	192	32	
8				32

Suppose the demand in month 8 in fact proves to be thirty-three units. Proceeding in the same way, the new total demand for the six months 3, 4, 5, 6, 7 and 8 is then:

$$192 - 29 + 33 = 196$$

And to obtain a forecast for month 9 we have:

Month (1)	Demand (2)	Total demand in last 6 months (3)	6 month moving average (4)	Forecast (5)
7	37	192	32	
8	33	196	32·67	32
9				32·67

Note that it is not essential to have both columns 4 and 5; both have been shown here only for the purpose of explanation.

With regard to the choice of time span, i.e. whether to employ a 3, 6 or 12 month moving average, there are a number of factors to consider. Averaging over a long time span such as twelve months will provide good smoothing of any random fluctuations in demand. On the other hand, a 12 month moving average will be slow to respond to any changes in the demand pattern. Where a more rapid response to changes in demand pattern is required and random fluctuations are not particularly pronounced, a shorter time span would be a better choice.

Trend correction

The moving average method assumes that the underlying mean is, for practical purposes, constant and fluctuations about this mean are random.

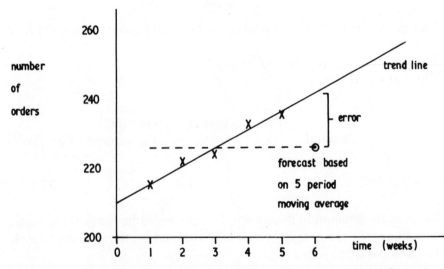

Fig. 4.2   Moving average: forecasting error due to presence of trend

In the presence of a pronounced trend the moving average will lag behind the trend simply because the moving average is an average of past data (see Figure 4.2).

Consider now the data shown in Table 4.2 and illustrated in Figure 4.3 on the monthly sales of polymer during the last twelve months.

Table 4.2

Monthly polymer sales

Month	Sales
1	33
2	34
3	37
4	34
5	41
6	44
7	50
8	46
9	47
10	52
11	45
12	55

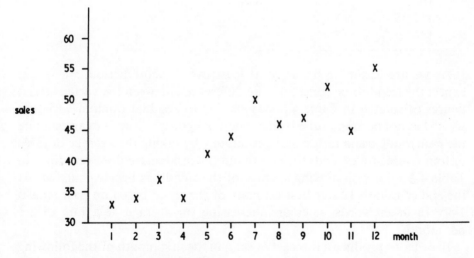

Fig. 4.3   Graph of polymer sales

This data clearly has a pronounced trend. If we take a 5 month moving average of the data, then each average will be an estimate of sales at the midpoint of the time period taken, i.e. half-way through the third month. We can indicate this by centering each moving average at the midpoint of the time period on which it is based. This is shown in the third column of Table 4.3. An estimate of the trend can then be obtained by calculating the difference between successive moving averages. This is shown in the fourth column of Table 4.3.

Table 4.3

Estimation of the trend using moving averages

Month (1)	Sales (2)	5 period MA (3)	Trend (4)	4 period MA of the trend (5)
1	33			
2	34			
3	37	35·8		
4	34	38·0	+2·2	
5	41	41·2	+3·2	2·45
6	44	43·0	+1·8	2·45
7	50	45·6	+2·6	1·70
8	46	47·8	+2·2	1·50
9	47	48·0	+0·2	
10	52	49·0	+1·0	
11	45			
12	55			

As we are assuming linearity, at least over a short period, we would expect the trend to be constant. The differences between the various trend figures calculated in Table 4.3 may be due to residual random variation which has not been smoothed out by the averaging process. We can estimate the underlying trend rather more accurately by taking the average of three or four consecutive trends to smooth out the residual random variation. In Table 4.3 a 4 period moving average of the trend has been calculated. At the end of month 12 our best estimate of the trend based on past data is 1·50. In other words, sales are increasing on average at a rate of 1·5 per month.

In order to produce a forecast of sales in the first month of the following year, the moving average line must be projected forward. The latest available moving average is 49·0. This is the average of the last five months' sales and therefore tells us the average monthly rate at the middle of that period, i.e. during month 10. To allow for this two month lag we must add twice the monthly trend to the latest moving average. This brings us up to date. Then a further one times the monthly trend must be added to project sales forward one month into the future. Thus, to obtain a forecast of sales next month, we must add three times the monthly trend to the latest moving average. A forecast for two months ahead would require four times the trend to be added and so on. An examination of Figure 4.4 will make this clear. Our forecast for the first month of the following year is:

$$49·0 + (3 \times 1·50) = 53·5$$

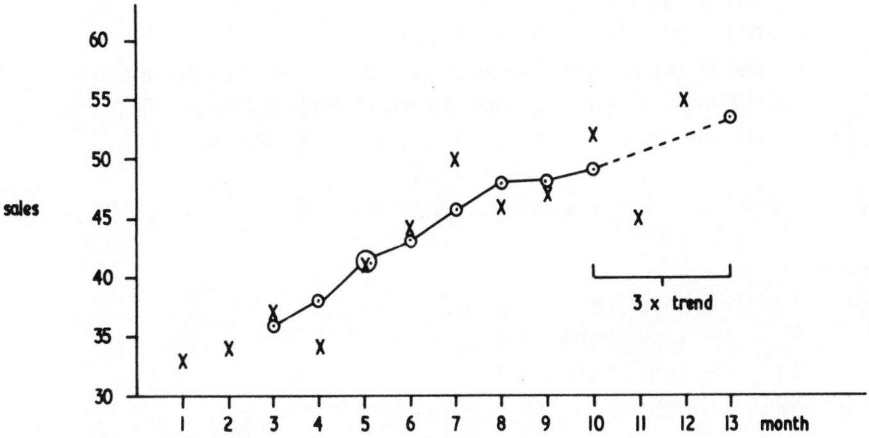

Fig. 4.4   Projection of trend line forward to month 13

Although this method of forecasting has the advantage of being relatively simple the estimation of the trend is very crude. If we look in detail at our method of calculating the trend in month 6, we see that the sum involves:

$$\frac{34 + 37 + 34 + 41 + 44}{5} - \frac{33 + 34 + 37 + 34 + 41}{5}$$

$$= \frac{44}{5} - \frac{33}{5} = 2·2$$

The data from months 2, 3 and 4 have no effect on the trend if it is calculated in this way. A more reliable method of estimating the trend is to fit a straight line to the past data and to obtain from this an estimate of the trend. This method will now be described in more detail.

Trend estimation using regression analysis

Instead of projecting forward the moving average line to obtain our forecast, we can fit a regression line to the past data and project this forward. The equation of the regression line is:

$$y - \bar{y} = b\,(x - \bar{x})$$

where

$y =$ the value of the item to be forecast, in this case sales, during a particular time period.

$x =$ the corresponding time period.

$b =$ the trend, in this case average increase in sales per month.

$\bar{y} =$ the mean of the y values for which data are available.

$\bar{x} =$ the mean of the x values for which data are available.

$$\bar{x} = \frac{\Sigma x}{n} \text{ and } \bar{y} = \frac{\Sigma y}{n}$$

where

Σ is shorthand for 'the sum of'

$\Sigma x =$ the sum of the x values

$\Sigma y =$ the sum of the y values

The best estimate of the trend is given by:

$$b = \frac{\Sigma xy - \dfrac{\Sigma x\,\Sigma y}{n}}{\Sigma x^2 - \dfrac{(\Sigma x)^2}{n}}$$

where

$n =$ number of pairs of values available

Σxy means multiply each x value by the corresponding y value and sum the results

Σx^2 means square each x value and sum the results.

As the trend is likely to change over time, only the more recent data can be used to estimate the trend. Table 4.4 shows a calculation of the regression line for the example which has just been considered using sales figures for the last five months. (The months have been renumbered to simplify the arithmetic.)

64

Table 4.4

Regression analysis using previous five months' sales

Month x	Sales y	xy	x^2
1	46	46	1
2	47	94	4
3	52	156	9
4	45	180	16
5	55	275	25
$\Sigma x = 15$	$\Sigma y = 245$	$\Sigma xy = 751$	$\Sigma x^2 = 55$

$$\bar{x} = \frac{15}{5} = 3{\cdot}0$$

$$\bar{y} = \frac{245}{5} = 49{\cdot}0$$

$$b = \frac{751 - \dfrac{15 \times 245}{5}}{55 - \dfrac{15 \times 15}{5}} = \frac{751 - 735}{55 - 45} = 1{\cdot}6$$

The equation of the regression line is:

$$y - 49{\cdot}0 = 1{\cdot}6 \,(x - 3{\cdot}0)$$
$$\text{i.e. } y = 44{\cdot}2 + 1{\cdot}6x$$

To obtain a forecast of sales for next month we just substitute $x = 6$ in the above equation.

i.e. Forecast $= 44{\cdot}2 + 1{\cdot}6 \times 6$
$= 53{\cdot}8$

Exponential smoothing

Both of the methods considered so far have two disadvantages:

1 All of the past data included in the calculation is given equal weighting when making the forecast. For example in a 12 month moving average, the demand twelve months ago contributes one-twelfth of its value to the forecast and has just the same weight as the most recent forecast. It is likely that more accurate forecasts would be produced by giving a higher weighting to the most recent data and a lower weighting to data from further into the past.

2 Provision must be made to store past data back as far as the extent of the time span of the calculation. This is a serious disadvantage in computer stock control applications when past demand data for each stock item must be held in the computer store at a substantial cost.

We now consider another method of forecasting, exponential smoothing, which has been developed in recent years and is rapidly increasing in popularity. It avoids the disadvantages of the forecasting methods previously discussed and is ideally suited to computer operation.

Exponential smoothing is based on a method of calculating the moving average in which the most recent sales figure is used to update the previous moving average.

$$\text{New average} = a \times \text{latest sales} + (1 - a) \times \text{previous average} \quad (4.1)$$

The quantity a is known as the *smoothing constant* and is a number which can be set to any value between 0 and 1. There is no simple way in which the best value for a can be calculated in any particular situation. The method usually used is to take a few years' historical data and compile forecasts using different values for a. These forecasts are then compared with the actual sales figures during the test period, and that value of a selected which has produced the most accurate forecasts. In most cases a value of a between 0·1 and 0·3 gives the best results.

It is more convenient to rewrite equation (1) as:

$$E_n = aS_n + (1 - a) E_{n-1} \quad (4.2)$$

where

E_n = exponentially weighted moving average (EWMA) this month, month n.

S_n = sales this month.

E_{n-1} = EWMA last month, month $n - 1$.

Suppose we wish to exponentially smooth the data in Table 4.1 using a smoothing constant, $a = 0·2$. In month 1:

$$E_1 = 0·2 \times S_1 + 0·8 \times E_0$$

So in order to get started we need an estimate of E_0. Average demand over the previous twelve months was 32·0. We shall use this as our estimate of E_0.

In month 1 demand was thirty-one:

$$\therefore \quad E_1 = \quad 0·2 \times 31 + 0·8 \times 32$$
$$= 31·8$$

As, in this case, we are assuming that the trend is zero, then this is our forecast of demand in month 2.

In fact, using the demand figures from Table 4.1, demand in month 2 proves to be twenty-nine units.

therefore

$$E_2 = 0.2 \times 29 + 0.8 \times 31.8$$
$$= 31.2$$

This is our forecast for month 3.

Then, when demand during month 3 proves to be thirty units,

$$E_3 = 0.2 \times 30 + 0.8 \times 31.2$$
$$= 31.0$$

and so on.

An alternative method of calculation

Equation (4.2) gave us:

$$E_n = aS_n + (1 - a) E_{n-1}$$

We can re-arrange the right hand side of the equation to give:

$$E_n = aS_n + E_{n-1} - aE_{n-1}$$
$$\text{i.e. } E_n = E_{n-1} + a(S_n - E_{n-1}) \tag{4.3}$$

This second form proves slightly quicker for calculation purposes. The part in brackets is the difference between the latest sales figure and the previous EWMA, i.e. the error of the EWMA as a forecast of sales. The calculations are as shown in Table 4.5 (the smoothing constant a is 0.2 as before).

Table 4.5

Calculation of exponentially weighted moving average

Month (n)	Demand (S_n)	Previous EWMA (E_{n-1})	Error $(S_n - E_{n-1})$	$0.2 \times$ error $= t_n$	New EWMA (E_n)
1	31	32.0	−1.0	−0.2	31.8
2	29	31.8	−2.8	−0.56	31.2
3	30	31.2	−1.2	−0.24	31.0
4	33	31.0	+2.0	+0.4	31.4
5	34	31.4	+2.6	+0.52	31.9
6	29	31.9	−2.9	−0.58	31.3
7	37	31.3	+5.7	+1.14	32.4
8	31	32.4	−1.4	−0.28	32.1
9	32	32.1	−0.1	−0.02	32.1

An additional advantage of this way of setting out calculations is that the error figures in the fourth column are of value in themselves. If the forecast is unbiased then these errors will be sometimes positive and sometimes negative, with the total of errors tending to zero. In the presence of a pronounced trend the EWMA tends to lag behind current demand, and in such cases errors will not sum to zero.

The structure of the exponentially weighted moving average

It is clear that the use of exponential smoothing will considerably reduce data storage requirements, as each stage in the calculation requires only three values: a, S_n and E_{n-1}. It is less obvious that this method of calculation will result in a weighted moving average. This can be best demonstrated as follows.

Suppose that we have decided to introduce exponential smoothing with a smoothing constant $a = 0.2$. A value for E_0 has been estimated so that, in month 1,

$$E_1 = 0.2S_1 + 0.8E_0 \tag{4.4}$$

In month 2

$$E_2 = 0.2S_2 + 0.8E_1$$

substituting equation (4.4)

$$E_2 = 0.2S_2 + 0.8 \times 0.2S_1 + (0.8)^2 E_0 \tag{4.5}$$

In month 3

$$E_3 = 0.2S_3 + 0.8E_2$$

substituting equation (4.5)

$$E_3 = 0.2S_3 + 0.8 \times 0.2S_2 + (0.8)^2 \times 0.2S_1 + (0.8)^3 E_0$$
$$= 0.2S_3 + 0.16S_2 + 0.128S_1 + 0.512E_0 \tag{4.6}$$

and so on.

In general

$$E_n = aS_n + a(1-a)S_{n-1} + a(1-a)^2 S_{n-2} + \ldots + a(1-a)^{n-1}S_1 + (1-a)^n E_0 \tag{4.7}$$

It can be seen that this method of calculation results in a weighted average of the sales figures with the weightings reducing for sales figures further into the past. There is a residual weighting associated with E_0 but this weighting will become relatively small after a few periods.

For example, for a smoothing constant of 0·2 the weighting of E_0 would reduce as follows:

$$0·8^2 = 0·640$$
$$0·8^3 = 0·512$$
$$0·8^4 = 0·410$$
$$0·8^5 = 0·328$$
$$0·8^6 = 0·262$$
$$0·8^7 = 0·210$$
$$0·8^8 = 0·168$$
$$0·8^9 = 0·134$$
$$0·8^{10} = 0·107$$

The weightings of the sales figures will be as shown in Table 4.6.

Table 4.6

Weightings for a smoothing constant of 0·2

Number of periods back	Weight given to that sales figure
1	0·2
2	0·16
3	0·128
4	0·102
5	0·082
6	0·066
7	0·052
8	0·042
etc.	

The series of weightings forms a mathematical progression called the exponential series. It can be shown that the sum of these weights if taken sufficiently far back, tends to unity.

As the size of the smoothing constant is increased, the emphasis on the most recent sales figures is increased. So one way of making the starting value E_0 less critical is to start off with a high value for the smoothing constant, say, $a = 0·5$. After five or six time periods the smoothing constant can be reduced to some lesser figure, say, $a = 0·2$.

With a smoothing of 0·5, the weighting of E_0 will reduce as follows:

$$0·5^2 = 0·25$$
$$0·5^3 = 0·125$$
$$0·5^4 = 0·062$$
$$0·5^5 = 0·031$$

$$0 \cdot 5^6 = 0 \cdot 016$$
$$0 \cdot 5^7 = 0 \cdot 008$$
$$0 \cdot 5^8 = 0 \cdot 004$$
$$0 \cdot 5^9 = 0 \cdot 002$$

The weights given to the demand figures will be as indicated in Table 4.7.

Table 4.7

Weightings for a smoothing constant of $0 \cdot 5$

Numbers of periods back	Weight given to that sales figure
1	0·5
2	0·25
3	0·125
4	0·062
5	0·031
6	0·016
7	0·008
8	0·004
etc.	

It can be seen that, with the larger smoothing constant, greater prominence is given to recent sales figures and the weighting tails off rapidly as one goes further into the past. Thus use of a higher value for the smoothing constant gives a more responsive forecasting system with the disadvantage of being over-sensitive to random fluctuations in the data.

Estimation of the trend using exponential smoothing

With the arithmetic moving average method of forecasting, we estimated the trend by subtracting successive moving averages. With exponential smoothing we can estimate the trend by subtracting successive exponentially weighted moving averages.

i.e.
$$t_n = E_n - E_{n-1} \tag{4.8}$$

where t_n is the current estimate of the trend.

Using equation (4.3)

$$t_n = E_{n-1} + a(S_n - E_{n-1}) - E_{n-1}$$
$$= a(S_n - E_{n-1}) \tag{4.9}$$

In the arithmetic moving average method, we estimated the future trend by taking an arbitrary average of the last three or four figures in the trend column. When exponential smoothing is being used, it is usual to take an exponentially weighted average of trend estimates. If T_n is the average trend at time period n, this may be expressed by the formula:

$$T_n = bt_n + (1 - b) T_{n-1} \qquad (4.10)$$

where b is the smoothing constant. b need not necessarily be the same value as a in the EWMA equation. In practice the best forecasts are obtained with values of b between 0·001 and 0·1.

An alternative version of equation (4.10) more useful for calculation is:

$$T_n = T_{n-1} + b (t_n - T_{n-1}) \qquad (4.11)$$

To illustrate the approach, the data from Table 4.2 have been exponentially smoothed using $a = 0.2$, $b = 0.1$, $E_0 = 25$ and $T_n = 2$. The results are shown in Table 4.8.

Table 4.8

Estimation of trend using exponential smoothing

n	S_n	E_{n-1}	$S_n - E_{n-1}$	$0.2(S_n - E_{n-1})$	E_n	t_n $= 0.2(S_n - E_{n-1})$	T_{n-1}	$t_n - T_{n-1}$	$0.1(t_n - T_{n-1})$	T_n
1	33	25	8	1·6	26·6					
2	34	26·6	7·4	1·48	28·1	1·48	2	−0·52	−0·052	1·95
3	37	28·1	8·9	1·78	29·9	1·78	1·95	−0·17	−0·017	1·93
4	34	29·9	4·1	0·82	30·7	0·82	1·93	−1·11	−0·111	1·82
5	41	30·7	10·3	2·06	32·8	2·06	1·82	+0·24	+0·024	1·84
6	44	32·8	11·2	2·24	35·0	2·24	1·84	+0·40	+0·04	1·88
7	50	35·0	15·0	3·00	38·0	3·00	1·88	+1·12	+0·112	1·99
8	46	38·0	8·0	1·60	39·6	1·60	1·99	−0·39	−0·039	1·95
9	47	39·6	7·4	1·48	41·1	1·48	1·95	−0·47	−0·047	1·90
10	52	41·1	10·9	2·18	43·3	2·18	1·90	+0·28	+0·028	1·93
11	45	43·3	1·7	0·34	43·6	0·34	1·93	−1·59	−0·159	1·77
12	55	43·6	11·4	2·28	45·9	2·28	1·77	+0·51	+0·051	1·82

You will notice that in Table 4.8 the current EWMA always lags behind the current sales level. It can be shown that the size of this lag is $((1 - a)/a)$ time periods.

To project the trend line forward, therefore, we must first add on $((1 - a)/a)$ times the estimated trend to bring it up to date, and then add on a further trend estimate for each period into the future we wish to go. These stages may be summarised in the formula:

$$F_{n+i} = E_n + \left(\frac{1 - a}{a}\right) T_n + i\, T_n \qquad (4.12)$$

where F_{n+i} is the forecast for i periods ahead.

When this is applied to the data in Table 4.8, the forecast for month 13 is:

$$F_{13} = 45 \cdot 9 + \left(\frac{1 - 0 \cdot 2}{0 \cdot 2}\right) \times 1 \cdot 82 + 1 \cdot 82$$
$$= 55 \cdot 0$$

Seasonal effects

Consider the following data (Consumer Expenditure on Footwear in £m. taken from Monthly Digest of Statistics).

Table 4.9

Quarterly expenditure on footwear (£m.)

Year	Quarter			
	1	2	3	4
1969	73	99	96	126
1970	81	114	108	148
1971	91	121	117	154
1972	106	131	135	175
1973	134	149		

Although the figures appear at first sight to vary tremendously, closer inspection reveals that they do so in a systematic way. First a *seasonal effect* can be identified. The fourth quarter figure is the largest, the first is the smallest, etc. Second there is a tendency for the figures to increase from year to year, i.e. a *trend*. In order to produce forecasts from these figures it is necessary to isolate and measure these two effects.

Estimation of seasonal effects

There are many ways in which seasonal effects can be estimated and a seasonal index produced. We shall illustrate one of the most commonly used methods with reference to the example given above. The first stage is to produce a new deseasonalised series by taking 4 period moving averages of the original series. This new series (see Table 4.10) has values which are centred half-way between two quarters. The next stage, therefore, is to produce a further series by taking 2 period moving averages of the 4 period moving average (see Table 4.10). The net result is a moving average of the original series over five periods where the weight given to each of the middle three periods is one-quarter and the weight given to the end periods is one-eighth.

Table 4.10

Deseasonalisation of data by taking moving averages

		Original data	4 Period MA	2 Period MA of 4 period MA
1969	1	73		
	2	99		
			98·5	
	3	96		99·5
			100·5	
	4	126		102·375
			104·25	
1970	1	81		105·75
			107·25	
	2	114		110·0
			112·75	
	3	108		114·0
			115·25	
	4	148		116·125
			117·0	
1971	1	91		118·125
			119·25	
	2	121		120·0
			120·75	
	3	117		122·625
			124·5	
	4	154		125·75
			127·0	
1972	1	106		129·25
			131·5	
	2	131		134·125
			136·75	
	3	135		140·25
			143·75	
	4	175		146·0
			148·25	
1973	1	134		
	2	149		

In the case of Consumer Expenditure on Footwear it is reasonable to assume that the seasonal effect is a *proportional effect,* i.e. that it increases or decreases the values in each quarter by a certain proportion. To estimate these proportions we divide the numbers in column 1 of Table 4.10 by those in column 3 and average the values obtained for each quarter (see Table 4.11).

Table 4.11

Estimation of proportional seasonal effects

	1969	1970	1971	1972	Average
1st Quarter		0·766	0·770	0·820	0·785
2nd Quarter		1·036	1·008	0·977	1·007
3rd Quarter	0·965	0·947	0·954	0·963	0·957
4th Quarter	1·231	1·275	1·225	1·199	1·232

Finally, to produce a *seasonal index,* the four numbers in the final column of Table 4.11 must be adjusted so that they average 1·0. In this case they already average 0·99525 so that the adjustment is carried out by dividing each one by this number (see Table 4.12, where figures have been rounded to two decimal places).

Table 4.12

Proportional seasonal effects adjusted to average 1·0

Quarter	Seasonal index
1	0·79
2	1·01
3	0·96
4	1·24

The interpretation of the index is straightforward. In the first quarter consumer expenditure on footwear is 21 per cent below that for an average quarter. In the second quarter, it is 1 per cent higher than that for an average quarter etc.

Two remarks should be made about the method given here:

1 In this example the seasonal pattern repeated itself every 4 periods so that a 4 period moving average was appropriate in order to remove all seasonal effects. If the data had been monthly a 12 period moving average would have been appropriate and so on.

2　An alternative to the proportional effects model given above is the additive effects model, where it is assumed that the seasonal effect produces constant (and not proportional) differences from the average in each time period. In practice the model is only rarely appropriate. When it is, the seasonal effects must be calculated by subtracting the numbers in column 3 of Table 4.10 from those in column 1 and then averaging the values obtained for each quarter. In the above example the seasonal effects would be:

1st Quarter　$-25 \cdot 04$
2nd Quarter　$+0 \cdot 63$
3rd Quarter　$-5 \cdot 09$
4th Quarter　$+28 \cdot 19$

(These can be normalised so that they add up to zero by adding a small fixed amount to each one.)

Preparing the forecast

Once the seasonal effects have been quantified, the trend must be estimated. Any of the three methods already described can be used.

1　Moving averages

In the example given above the four most recent trend figures are 4·5, 5·25, 7·0, 4·5, giving an average trend of 5·3 per quarter. The most recent moving average is 148·25. This lags 1½ quarters behind the current quarter and therefore 2½ quarters behind the next quarter for which a forecast is required. A projection of the trend to the next quarter therefore gives:

$$148 \cdot 25 + 2 \cdot 5 \times 5 \cdot 3 = 161 \cdot 5$$

and a forecast is obtained by multiplying this by the seasonal index for the quarter, i.e.

Forecast $= 161 \cdot 5 \times 0 \cdot 96 = 155$ (to the nearest whole number)

2　Regression

A linear or polynomial regression can be carried out on the original data to project trends into the future. The projected trend is then multiplied by the seasonal index to produce forecasts. This method is not often used in stock control but can be quite successful in, for example, forecasting the market size of a recently introduced product where past experience leads one to believe that a certain type of growth curve is appropriate.

3 Exponential smoothing

Exponential smoothing cannot be used directly on the data when seasonal effects are present. As the weights given to each time period are different, the forecast would be biased according to the seasonal effect experienced in the most recent time period. However, if the series is deseasonalised by first dividing by the seasonal indices, exponential smoothing can be applied. In the above example the last few terms of the deseasonalised series are:

$$\ldots 141\cdot3,\ 169\cdot6,\ 147\cdot9$$

Exponential smoothing can be used to forecast the next term in this series and the seasonal index can then be applied to this in order to produce a forecast for the original series.

This method is frequently used when it is necessary to control the stocks of large numbers of items, each exhibiting similar seasonal sales patterns. A single sales pattern is calculated once every few years and this is then applied to all products. This method has the advantage that the amount of data stored either manually or on computer at any one time is kept to a minimum.

Monitoring forecasting systems

One of the most difficult situations to cope with in forecasting is a sudden change in trend. Initially it is difficult to distinguish between a genuine change in trend and random variation. As a result, all forecasting systems show some delay before responding to sudden changes, the delay resulting in an increase in forecasting error.

It is therefore important that forecasts are continually monitored so that sudden increases in forecasting error can be investigated. In most cases it is possible to estimate from knowledge of external factors whether there is a genuine change in trend and, if so, how long the new trend is likely to be maintained.

Trigg's tracking signal

Trigg has suggested a method of monitoring using a 'tracking signal' which provides a measure of the forecasting error.

$$\text{Trigg's tracking signal} = \frac{\text{exponentially smoothed error in period } t}{\text{mean absolute deviation in period } t}$$

$$= \frac{\bar{e}_t}{\text{MAD}_t}$$

$\bar{e}_t$ is obtained by exponentially smoothing the forecasting errors over successive time periods.

$$\bar{e}_t = ae_t + (1 - a)\,\bar{e}_{t-1}$$

MAD_t is obtained by exponentially smoothing the absolute forecasting errors, (i.e. the calculation of MAD_t is the same as that for $\bar{e}_t$ except that e_t is regarded as positive even when the forecasting error is negative) the absolute value of e_t is denoted by the symbol $|e_t|$.

$$MAD_t = a|e_t| + (1 - a)\,MAD_{t-1}$$

Trigg's tracking signal has a range of -1 to $+1$. When the forecasting system is in control, positive and negative forecasting errors will tend to cancel each other out, making $\bar{e}_t$ very small. Under these conditions the tracking signal will be close to zero.

If there is a sudden change in trend, then the forecasts will lag behind the actual data, leading to a series of forecasting errors all with the same sign (see Figure 4.5). This will lead to a large positive or negative value for $\bar{e}_t$ and the tracking signal will approach $+1$ or -1 depending on the sign of $\bar{e}_t$.

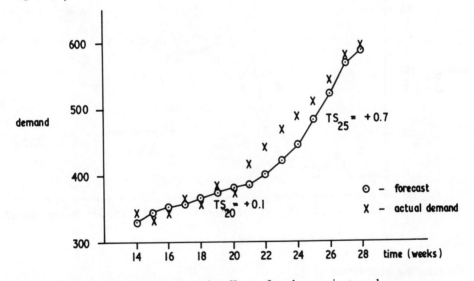

Fig. 4.5   Trigg's tracking signal: effect of a change in trend

Adaptive forecasting

Adaptive forecasting is a method of forecasting in which the size of the forecasting error is used to alter the sensitivity of the forecast to recent

77

data. Thus, in the example illustrated in Figure 4.5, when the forecasting error suddenly increased in week 21 the weighting of recent demand figures would be increased. This would rapidly bring the forecast back in line with the new trend and normal weightings could then be restored.

A simple method of adaptive forecasting has been suggested by Trigg and Leach. This method uses exponential smoothing of the data with a smoothing constant a, equal to the absolute value of Trigg's tracking signal. Using this method, when forecasts start to go out of control due to sudden changes in average demand the smoothing constant is automatically increased. This gives more weight to recent data so that the forecast rapidly moves back in line with actual demand. Once this happens the smoothing constant is automatically reduced again to prevent the forecast being unduly sensitive to small random fluctuations in demand. Figure 4.6 shows how accurate forecasts produced by this method can be even in situations where sales fluctuate violently.

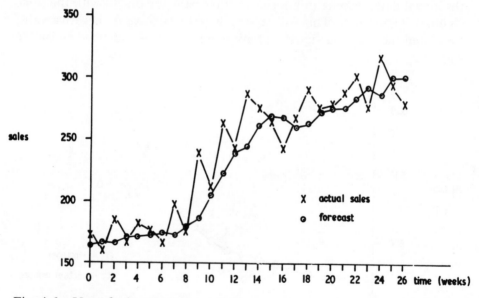

Fig. 4.6   Use of adaptive forecasting

Forecasting in practice

Forecasting is inevitably very difficult. The forecaster has to try to combine a number of different types of information, some quantitative and some qualitative. He must take into account the differences in reliability of the various sorts of information and finally arrive at a forecast which is, hopefully, not too far from reality.

While quantitative methods of forecasting can be very helpful, their cost tends to rise extremely rapidly with increasing complexity. It is important that the cost of producing an increase in forecasting accuracy is not greater than the value of the benefits resulting from the improvement. A rough measure of the upper limit for expenditure on forecasting can be obtained by estimating the additional benefits which would result from perfect forecasts. This can then be used as a guide to an acceptable level of expenditure in order to achieve a given percentage increase in forecasting accuracy.

In order to forecast effectively, an important preliminary is the determination of those areas where accurate forecasts are of vital importance to the organisation. Forecasting effort can then be concentrated on these areas while simpler and cheaper techniques can be used elsewhere. For each forecast the most appropriate technique must be selected, taking into account the data available, the required accuracy, the potential value of the forecast and how far into the future it is desired to forecast. Whatever technique is selected, the final forecast must be based on a combination of the technique and the knowledge and experience of the managers concerned.

In order to use forecasts properly the manager must have a basic understanding of the techniques being used and their limitations. He must have some idea of the accuracy of the forecast in order to know how much reliance to place on the forecast. The manager should never blindly accept forecasts. He should always ask himself whether they look reasonable in the light of his own knowledge. If the forecasts do not look reasonable he should check with the forecaster to ensure that all the relevant external factors have been allowed for.

Provided that forecasts are based on a proper blend of experience and techniques, then substantial improvements in forecasting accuracy can be achieved and this should produce a corresponding improvement in the quality of management decision making.

References

Box, G.E.P. and Jenkins, R.M., *Time Series Forecasting and Control,* Holden-Day, 1968.

Brown, R.G., *Statistical Forecasting for Inventory Control,* McGraw-Hill, 1959.

Brown, R.G., *Smoothing, Forecasting and Prediction of Discrete Time Series,* Prentice-Hall, 1962.

ICI, *Mathematical Trend Curves: an Aid to Forecasting*, ICI Monograph no. 1, Oliver & Boyd, 1964.

ICI, *Short term Forecasting*, ICI Monograph no. 2, Oliver & Boyd, 1964.

ICI, *Cumulative Sum Techniques*, ICI Monograph no. 3, Oliver & Boyd, 1964.

Institute of Cost and Works Accountants, *An Introduction to Business Forecasting*, 1960.

Morrell, J., *Business Forecasting for Finance and Industry*, Gower Press, 1969.

Trigg, D.W., 'Monitoring a Forecasting System', *Operational Research Quarterly*, vol. 15, no. 3, 1964, p. 271.

Trigg, D.W. and Leach, A.G., 'Exponential Smoothing with Adaptive Response Rate', *Operational Research Quarterly*, vol. 18, no. 1, 1967, p. 53.

Winters, P.R., 'Forecasting Sales by Exponentially Weighted Moving Averages', *Management Science*, vol. 6, 1960, p. 324.

Exercises

1 The following figures are the numbers of driving tests conducted in the UK (in 100,000s) for the years 1967–74:

$$21.9, 20.4, 17.1, 17.1, 15.9, 15.4, 15.3, 16.8$$

Calculate 3 year and 5 year moving averages. Given that the exponentially weighted moving average (smoothing constant = 0.3) calculated in 1966 was 22.0 calculate exponentially weighted moving averages for subsequent years.

2 The following figures relate to the sales of heating oil.

	Year 1	Year 2	Year 3
1st Quarter	320	345	365
2nd Quarter	185	200	210
3rd Quarter	215	230	240
4th Quarter	395	420	440

Estimate the seasonal effects using first a 'proportional effects model' and second an 'additive effects model'. Use the moving average method to produce a forecast for the first quarter of year 4.

3 The following data represents the weekly sales of an item over the last twenty weeks.

Week	Sales	Week	Sales
1	177	11	263
2	182	12	236
3	123	13	208
4	216	14	269
5	212	15	298
6	240	16	300
7	203	17	278
8	204	18	285
9	220	19	277
10	180	20	298

In order to control production, a forecast is made at the end of each week for the following week's sales. In the past, forecasts have been based on a simple moving average taken over just two weeks, even though there are severe weekly fluctuations in sales. It has been proposed that forecasting accuracy could be improved by using some form of exponential smoothing.

Analyse the accuracy of the present method of forecasting and determine whether any improvement would result from the introduction of exponential smoothing. (Suitable starting values for exponential smoothing are $E_0 = 165$, $T_0 = 5$.)

4 Use the following comparison of actual sales and forecast sales to calculate Trigg's tracking signal month by month.

Month	Actual sales	Forecast sales
1	28	30
2	33	30
3	29	31
4	31	30
5	31	30
6	42	30
7	44	32
8	45	34
9	47	37
10	50	41
11	51	45
12	53	50

Use starting values of $\bar{e}_0 = 0.2$
$$MAD_0 = 2.0$$
What is the reason for the changes in Trigg's tracking signal over the 12 month period?

5   A company issues factory output statistics for each calendar month. Analysis reveals that for all factories output in December and February is consistently low. December is approximately 20 per cent below the average for all months and February is approximately 8 per cent below the average for all months. What reason can you give for this? How would you allow for this effect in your forecasting method?

6   A small mail order business sells kits of furniture for home assembly. Sales are growing rapidly, as can be seen from the data on number of orders received per week for the last twelve weeks. The number of orders received during weeks 11 and 12 are low due to a postal strike which lasted from Tuesday in week 11 up to and including Thursday in week 12. The strike is now over and the Post Office have said that all of the backlog should be cleared within a week.

Week	Number of orders received
1	196
2	208
3	224
4	214
5	257
6	247
7	256
8	262
9	286
10	287
11	61
12	132

How would you allow for the effect of the strike when forecasting the future level of orders. What is your forecast of number of orders received in week 13?

Case C   Superstar

Charles Robinson was the buyer for the toy department of a large department store. It was the end of October and the Christmas rush was really starting to build up. One product which was selling particularly well was a new game called Superstar, which had been brought on to the market by Vista Limited at the beginning of August.

The game is for two players and is played on a star-shaped board. Each player attempts to move one of his pieces to the centre of the board while preventing his opponent from doing so by placing obstacles on the board. The first player to reach the centre of the board is the winner. Although it was marketed as a children's game, the strategic element of the game exercised a fascination for all ages and many adults were buying sets for their own use.

When the game had been first launched Robinson had recognised that the game could have a major impact, provided it caught on. He had therefore placed an initial order for 400. As over 250 had already been sold, it was now necessary to place a further order. He checked weekly sales of the game so far (Exhibit 1), but it was still rather early to gain a clear indication of total pre-Christmas sales. He decided that it might be useful to talk to John Wilson, the manager of the toy department, before deciding on the order quantity.

Robinson: John, I have been giving some thought to our final Christmas ordering and I'm not sure what to do about Superstar. Sales so far have been encouraging, but do you think it will be really big?

Wilson: Yes, I think it's going to be a real winner. Vista have a special Superstar TV advertising campaign due to start in two weeks' time. Once that gets under way sales should really rocket.

Robinson: The problem is, how high will sales go? If we over-order we'll have stocks left on our hands and there's not much point in holding them over till next Christmas. I hear that Vista already have a new version of Superstar which they plan to market for next Christmas.

Wilson: It's a pity we have no pattern of sales from last Christmas to provide a comparison. That's the problem with new products. There's no past data, so forecasts have to be based on guesswork. Just to give you an idea you could have a look at sales of Epsilon last year. That was our biggest selling boxed game last Christmas.

Robinson: Thanks, I'll do that. If you had to put a number on it what would be your forecast of total Christmas sales of Superstar?

Wilson: Well, my usual rule of thumb is that total sales are six times sales up to the end of week 43. Let me see, that would give a total sales figure of about 1,600. But that would make it the biggest seller we've ever had. I suppose there's no way of ordering a few now and then topping up in a few weeks' time when we have a better idea of how sales are going?

Robinson: No, I've just been speaking to Vista on the telephone. They are still taking orders, but stocks are running down fast and for orders placed after the end of this week they cannot guarantee delivery before Christmas.

Wilson: Well, if this is our last chance to place an order I'll stick my neck out and say that we'll sell 1,200 altogether. We've had 400 already so that would mean ordering another 800. I know I said 1,600 a few minutes ago, but I can't see us selling that many. Anyway I'd rather err on the safe side and refuse a few customers than have the problems of getting rid of unsold stocks after Christmas.

Robinson: If we do over-order could we get rid of the unsold sets in the January sales?

Wilson: You might unload one or two but that's all. Nobody buys games in January. However, if sales are lower than we expect, then we could reduce the price for the last few weeks just before Christmas. I don't like doing it because it upsets customers who bought earlier, but I'll do it if it's the only way of getting rid of the unsold stocks.

Charles Robinson returned to his office and asked his secretary to check through last year's sales records and extract a week by week summary of total sales of boxed games during the Christmas period for the previous year. He also asked for similar information for each of the three best selling boxed games separately (Exhibit 2).

He checked on the discount arrangements which he had negotiated with Vista and found that the wholesale price was £1.30 with a 5 per cent discount for orders of 100 or more and a 10 per cent discount for orders of 400 or more.

The game was being sold at £1.95. The same price was being charged at the other large stores in the town. It seemed likely that any price cut would lead to similar price cuts elsewhere.

A short while later Robinson's secretary brought him the information for which he had asked, together with a summary of annual boxed game sales for the previous five years (Exhibit 3). He then had to reach a firm decision on the number of Superstar games to be ordered.

Assignment

Suggest how Mr Robinson should arrive at a forecast of total Superstar sales. What additional data should he collect? What is your forecast of total pre-Christmas sales of Superstar?

Exhibit 1

Weekly sales of Superstar

Week	Number of sets	Sales value (£)
31	6	11·70
32	1	1·95
33	2	3·90
34	4	7·80
35	5	9·75
36	8	15·60
37	12	23·40
38	16	31·20
39	21	40·95
40	27	52·65
41	39	76·05
42	54	105·30
43	68	132·60

Exhibit 2

Previous weekly sale of three boxed games

Week	Epsilon (£1.25)		Capture (£1.50)		Self-sufficiency (£2.95)		Sales of all boxed games (£)
	No. of sets	Sales value (£)	No. of sets	Sales value (£)	No. of sets	Sales value (£)	
35	3	3·75	2	3·00	1	2·95	247·35
36	4	5·00	2	3·00	0	0·00	256·70
37	4	5·00	1	1·50	3	8·85	318·45
38	6	7·50	4	6·00	4	11·80	553·65
39	7	8·75	6	9·00	6	17·70	775·70
40	12	15·00	9	13·50	5	14·75	994·10
41	19	23·75	14	21·00	9	26·55	1,637·35
42	26	32·50	20	30·00	11	32·45	2,229·00
43	41	51·25	27	40·50	17	50·15	2,672·15
44	50	62·50	33	49·50	20	59·00	3,143·00
45	48	60·00	40	60·00	26	76·70	3,854·50
46	66	82·50	39	58·50	31	91·45	4,196·60
47	71	88·75	58	87·00	37	109·15	4,739·50
48	82	102·50	61	91·50	40	118·00	5,382·05
49	83	103·75	62	93·00	45	132·75	5,947·35
50	92	115·00	74	111·00	55	162·25	6,638·75
51	90	112·50	65	97·50	43	126·85	6,246·90
Total	704		517		353		49,833·10

Exhibit 3

Boxed game sales over previous five years

Year	Sales (£)	Retail price index
1	29,755	140·2
2	33,968	153·4
3	36,427	164·3
4	41,623	179·4
5	49,833	208·2
this year	–	258·7*

*Estimated.

5 Simulation

In Chapter 2 the different types of quantitative model used in problem solving were introduced and the various methods of solution discussed. It was pointed out that, while mathematical optimising techniques can be used for the solution of some problems, there are many problems which cannot be solved in this way. This is because most real systems involve a large number of interacting factors whose inter-relationships are too complex.

Even in situations where a solution can be obtained, a number of simplifying assumptions must be made. This means that the solution will only be an approximation to the true optimal solution and in cases where some of the assumptions are not valid the discrepancy may be considerable.

An alternative method of analysis is simulation. Using a suitable model, it is possible to simulate the behaviour of any system under a specified set of operating conditions, taking into account all the factors relevant to the problem. The simulation can then be repeated under various operating conditions and the behaviour of the simulation model used to predict the best operating rules for the real system.

Simulation using past data

Let us consider a very simple example. Suppose a factor has the following stock control procedure:

    1 In January calculate average weekly demand for each item over the last twelve months.

    2 Over the next twelve months, re-order an item whenever the stock level falls below 2 × average demand during the lead-time, based on the demand calculated in step 1.

    3 For each item, the re-order quantity is 10 × the average weekly demand calculated in step 1.

The stock control manager believes he can reduce his overall costs by introducing the following modified stock control procedure:

    1 In January, calculate average weekly demand for each item over the last twelve months.

    2 Over the next twelve months, re-order an item whenever the stock level falls below average lead-time demand

$$+ 2 \times \sqrt{\text{average lead-time demand}}$$

3 For each item, the re-order quantity is

$$40 \times \sqrt{\frac{\text{average weekly demand}}{\text{unit price}}}$$

The works manager believes that this new procedure will increase the number of stockouts and may increase overall costs. One way of testing whether the proposed procedure would be an improvement is to simulate what would have happened over the last twelve months if the new procedure had been in operation.

Consider just one stock item, type WXA 231–C
Average weekly usage = 4·5 units
Lead-time   = 9 weeks
Unit price   = £20

Present stock control procedure
Re-order level $= 2 \times 9 \times 4\cdot5 = 81$
Re-order quantity $= 10 \times 4\cdot5 \quad = 45$

Proposed stock control procedure
Re-order level $= 9 \times 4\cdot5 + 2 \times \sqrt{9 \times 4\cdot5} = 53$

Re-order quantity $= 40 \times \sqrt{\dfrac{4\cdot5}{20}} \qquad = 19$

Table 5.1 shows the actual weekly usage over the last twelve months together with the stock variation with the present stock control procedure. Alongside is shown the stock variation which would have occurred if the proposed procedure had been in operation over the same period. The stock level at the start of the period was ninety-three.

Cost of placing an order   = £2
Stockholding cost   = 0·15 × average stock value
Cost of running out of stock = 0·5 × value of items demanded during period out of stock
Unit price   = £20

Present stock control procedure
Over the last 52 weeks
Number of orders placed = 5
Number of items which could not be met from stock = 0

Average stock level $= \dfrac{3360}{52} = 64\cdot62$

Table 5.1
Comparison of stock levels under present and proposed ordering rules

Present method				Proposed method			Present method				Proposed method		
Weekly demand	Stock level	Stock + orders	Orders	Stock level	Stock + orders	Orders	Weekly demand	Stock level	Stock + orders	Orders	Stock level	Stock + orders	Orders
	93	93		93	93		8	77	77	order	25	63	
2	91	91		91	91		4	73	118		21	59	
5	86	86		86	86		9	64	109		12	50	order
9	77	77	order	77	77		1	63	108		11	68	
2	75	120		75	75		6	57	102		24	62	receipt
9	66	111		66	66		5	52	97		19	57	
4	62	107		62	62		6	46	91		13	51	order
4	58	103		58	58		6	40	85		7	64	
1	57	102		57	57		4	36	81	order	22	60	receipt
0	57	102		57	57		6	75	120	receipt	16	54	
3	54	99		54	54		8	67	112		8	46	order
0	54	99		54	54		6	61	106		21	59	receipt
6	93	93	receipt	48	48	order	5	56	101		16	54	
6	87	87		42	61		2	54	99		14	52	order
8	79	79	order	34	53	order	7	47	92		7	61	
0	79	124		34	72		2	45	90		24	62	receipt
2	77	122		32	70		7	38	83		17	55	
4	73	118		28	66		8	75	75	order receipt	9	47	order
4	69	114		24	62		1	74	119		8	65	
2	67	112		22	60		9	65	110		18	56	receipt
4	63	108		18	56		6	59	104		12	50	order
0	63	108		37	56	receipt	9	50	95		3	60	
9	54	99		28	47	order	0	50	95		22	60	receipt
3	96	96	receipt	44	63	receipt	4	46	91		18	56	
0	96	96		44	63		5	41	86		13	51	
5	91	91		39	58		1	40	85		12	50	
6	85	85		33	52	order							

Total annual cost $= 5 \times 2 + 64 \cdot 62 \times 20 \times 0 \cdot 15$
$$= 10 + 193 \cdot 86$$
$$= £203 \cdot 86$$

Proposed stock control procedure

Over the last 52 weeks

Number of orders placed $= 10$

Number of items which could not be met from stock $= 0$

Average stock level $= \dfrac{1636}{52} = 31 \cdot 46$

Total annual cost $= 10 \times 2 + 31 \cdot 46 \times 20 \times 0 \cdot 15$
$$= 20 + 94 \cdot 38$$
$$= £114 \cdot 38$$

It therefore appears from the simulation that introduction of the proposed stock control procedure will substantially reduce overall costs. However, this simulation raises a number of important points.

Starting conditions

The choice of a starting stock level of ninety-three units was extremely unrealistic in the case of the proposed stock control procedure. If we wish to make a fair comparison between the two procedures we should compare them when both have settled down to a normal pattern of working. This can be done by using starting conditions which are known to be typical for the particular method being simulated. Alternatively we could start the simulation with arbitrary starting conditions and then discard the early part of the simulation up to the point where a steady state is reached.

In the stock control example, we might decide that it would take up to twenty-six weeks to settle down to a normal pattern. We would then discard the first twenty-six weeks' data and our results would be as follows:

Present stock control procedure
Over weeks 27 to 52

    Number of orders placed = 3

    Number of items which could not be met from stock = 0

    Average stock level $= \dfrac{1451}{26} = 55{\cdot}81$

Over a year we can therefore expect an average of six orders placed and an average stock level of 55·81.

    Total annual cost $= 6 \times 2 + 55{\cdot}81 \times 20 \times 0{\cdot}15$
$$= 12 + 167{\cdot}43$$
$$= £179{\cdot}43$$

Proposed stock control procedure
Over weeks 27 to 52

    Number of orders placed = 6

    Number of items which could not be met from stock = 0

    Average stock level $= \dfrac{392}{26} = 15{\cdot}08$

Over a year we can therefore expect an average of twelve orders placed and an average stock level of 15·08.

    Total annual cost $= 12 \times 2 + 15{\cdot}08 \times 20 \times 0{\cdot}15$
$$= 24 + 45{\cdot}24$$
$$= £69{\cdot}24$$

Although the total annual cost figures have changed, the proposed stock control procedure is still clearly superior to the present method.

Length of simulation

The conclusion we have reached in the previous paragraph is based on results over a period of just twenty-six weeks. This is too short a period to be representative of the long-run performance of either of the two methods under consideration, so that the results obtained are only approximate.

In the case of simulation based on past data the length of the simulation will be limited to the period for which past data is available. Later we shall introduce a method of simulation which can be extended over as long a period as we wish and at that stage the question of length of simulation will be discussed in more detail.

The optimum solution

In an optimising model, such as one of the linear programming models discussed in Chapter 3, attention is centred on the determination of 'the optimal solution'. A simulation model is different in that it can only indicate which of the alternatives actually considered is the best. For example, it might well be possible to suggest a stock control procedure which is an improvement on both of the methods just considered and this could be tested by simulating this third method using the same weekly demand figures as before. Even this might not be the optimum. There might be another alternative which is even better. The simulation method on its own gives no guidelines here.

Because of this difficulty, a common approach is to arrive at what appears to be an optimal solution by some other method and then to confirm this by using simulation to compare the apparent optimal solution with reasonable alternatives.

Monte Carlo simulation

In the stock control example we were able to simulate the behaviour of the alternatives under consideration using past data. In many situations past data will not be available in the required detail. Even when past records are available they may not cover a long enough period for the simulation results to be useful. In such circumstances a method of simulation called Monte Carlo simulation is used.

Consider the following problem.

Provision of delivery bays

Lorries arrive at a goods inwards department at irregular intervals. Each lorry takes one hour to unload but there are only two delivery bays. If all the bays are occupied when a lorry arrives, then the lorry has to wait until a bay is free. For each lorry there is a charge of £5 per hour from the time of arrival to the time when unloading is completed. Construction of an extra delivery bay is being considered in order to reduce vehicle waiting time. How can the reduction in waiting time be determined?

One method of dealing with this problem is to simulate the behaviour of the system with two bays and then with three bays, comparing the average waiting time per lorry in each case. In order to carry out the simulations we need to know the sequence of lorry arrival times over a representative period, say three months. This data is unlikely to be already available. The information could be collected by carrying out a continuous time study over the three months but this would be prohibitively expensive. We must therefore develop an alternative method of generating the sequence of lorry arrival times.

Although the lorries will arrive at random intervals we shall suppose that the probability distribution of time between lorry arrivals is expected to remain the same over the three month period. The probability distribution can be constructed fairly quickly by recording times between successive lorry arrivals over a few days.

Suppose that the probability distribution of lorry inter-arrival time is as shown in Table 5.2. The table tells us the frequency of occurrence of each range of inter-arrival times. We require a random sequence of inter-arrival times which fits this distribution over a reasonable period. First we need to replace each range of inter-arrival times by a single value. We can do this by rounding to 5 minutes all inter-arrival times from 0 up to 10 minutes, rounding to 15 minutes all inter-arrival times from 10 up to 20 minutes, and so on.

Then one approach to generating a random sequence of lorry inter-arrival times is to take 100 slips of paper. Write 5 minutes on 26 slips, 15 minutes on 20 slips, 25 minutes on 16 slips, etc. so that the slips are in the same proportions as the distribution of inter-arrival times. Place the slips in a hat, mix well and select one at random. If this slip has twenty-five minutes written on it then the first lorry will arrive twenty-five minutes after the start of the simulation. Replace the slip, shake well again and select another slip at random. If this has five minutes written on it then the next lorry will arrive five minutes after the first. By continuing in this way we could construct the sequence of lorry arrival times shown in Table 5.3.

Table 5.2

Distribution of time between successive lorry arrivals

Lorry inter-arrival times	Frequency	Probability = $\dfrac{\text{Frequency}}{50}$
0 up to 10 min.	13	0·26
10 up to 20 min.	10	0·20
20 up to 30 min.	8	0·16
30 up to 40 min.	5	0·10
40 up to 50 min.	4	0·08
50 up to 60 min.	3	0·06
60 up to 70 min.	2	0·04
70 up to 80 min.	2	0·04
80 up to 90 min.	1	0·02
90 up to 100 min.	1	0·02
100 up to 110 min.	1	0·02
	50	1·00

Table 5.3

Lorry arrival times generated by random sampling using slips of paper

Time between successive lorry arrivals (min.)	Time from start of simulation to arrival of lorry (min.)
25	25
5	30
65	95
35	130
35	165
15	180
35	215
15	230
15	245
25	270
5	275

This method of sampling from a distribution is called the Monte Carlo method. The sequence generated will be random but it will, in the long-run, contain the same proportions of the various inter-arrival times as the original distribution. The method makes it possible to extend the length of the simulation as much as we wish by generating a further sequence of inter-arrival times. Also the data on which the method is based can be collected relatively cheaply.

The precise sampling method which has been suggested is of course clumsy and it is difficult to ensure thorough mixing of the slips. A better method of achieving the same result is to use random numbers.

Random numbers are sets of digits where each digit has an equal probability of occurring. Tables of random numbers are available (see Table 5.8) and a section from a random number table is shown in Table 5.5.

If we consider two-digit random numbers, there are 100 such numbers, 00–99, each with an equal probability of occurring. We can therefore use the numbers 00–99 instead of the 100 slips of paper. We allocate the first 26 numbers, 00–25, to correspond to an inter-arrival time of 5 minutes, the next 20 numbers, 26–45, to correspond to an inter-arrival time of 15 minutes, and so on. This allocation is simplified if the probabilities in the distribution are converted to cumulative probabilities. (See Table 5.4.)

Table 5.4
Random number allocation

Lorry inter-arrival times (min.)	Probability	Cumulative probability	Random numbers
5	0·26	0·26	00–25
15	0·20	0·46	26–45
25	0·16	0·62	46–61
35	0·10	0·72	62–71
45	0·08	0·80	72–79
55	0·06	0·86	80–85
65	0·04	0·90	86–89
75	0·04	0·94	90–93
85	0·02	0·96	94–95
95	0·02	0·98	96–97
105	0·02	1·00	98–99
	1·00		

In Table 5.4 the numbers 00–99 have been allocated to lorry inter-arrival times in the same proportions as the original distribution. We can now read off a sequence of two-digit random numbers from Table 5.5 recording the corresponding lorry inter-arrival times and be sure that the sequence will be random and will fit the original distribution.

Table 5.5

Random numbers

74	35	59	44	11	26	78	60	91	90	05	43
22	38	32	08	⃝41	91	14	63	31	15	40	27
84	34	07	60	34	26	80	79	88	64	30	86
21	88	73	30	20	39	04	10	96	49	85	36
04	36	56	62	78	08	98	52	98	09	68	03
12	33	22	47	16	96	20	79	42	48	56	34
35	49	27	91	80	33	58	12	77	71	37	70
57	00	56	82	46	06	88	73	68	13	76	23
54	85	56	76	07	96	83	44	30	90	30	16
48	62	55	32	24	40	58	78	52	35	48	70

To read off a sequence of random numbers, choose a starting point and then select numbers in some sensible order (e.g. by working along rows or down columns). The random numbers used in Table 5.6 have been obtained from Table 5.5 by starting with the number which is ringed, continuing down that column and then down the next column etc.

Table 5.6

Use of random numbers to generate lorry arrival times

Random number	Lorry inter-arrival time (min.)	Time from start of simulation to arrival of lorry (min.)
41	15	15
34	15	30
20	5	35
78	45	80
16	5	85
80	55	140
46	25	165
07	5	170
24	5	175
26	15	190
91	75	265
26	15	280

A typical sequence of lorry arrival times having been generated, the operation of the delivery bays can be simulated. To do this we need more information on the working arrangements of the despatch department. The relevant details are summarised below.

1 The working day is 08.00 hours to 17.00 hours.
2 Lorries only arrive between these times. If any lorries are still awaiting unloading at 17.00 hours work continues until all the lorries have been unloaded. No lorries have to wait overnight.
3 There is a lunch break from 12.00 hours to 13.00 hours and tea breaks from 10.00 hours to 10.15 hours and 15.00 hours to 15.15 hours. Any lorries being unloaded when a break time occurs have to wait until the end of the break for completion.
4 The basic wage is for an 8 hour working day. Any work done after 17.00 hours is paid as overtime. There is no Saturday or Sunday working.

Table 5.7 shows simulation of two days' operation under these conditions, first with the existing two bays and then with three bays. The same sequence of lorry arrival times has been used in both simulations so that any differences can be attributed to the effect of the extra bay.

The following results were obtained.

Operating with two delivery bays
Total lorry waiting time + unloading time for day 1 = 3,110 minutes
Total lorry waiting time + unloading time for day 2 = 1,475 minutes

	4,585 minutes
Total overtime hours worked on day 1	= 4 hours 45 minutes
Total overtime hours worked on day 2	= 3 hours 20 minutes
	8 hours 05 minutes

Operating with three delivery bays
Total lorry waiting time + unloading time for day 1 = 1,590 minutes
Total lorry waiting time + unloading time for day 2 = 1,100 minutes

	2,690 minutes
Total overtime hours worked on day 1	= 1 hour 15 minutes
Total overtime hours worked on day 2	= 1 hour 35 minutes
	2 hours 50 minutes

In order to compare these two alternatives we need to estimate the various costs involved. We shall adopt a very simplistic view and assume that the cost of the new bay can be expressed as a daily cost covering depreciation and interest charges. There will also be the hourly cost of operating each bay, consisting mainly of labour costs, and there will be the charge made for the time each lorry is on the premises.

Cost of new bay $= £12$ per day
Operating cost per bay $= £5$ per hour of day work
Operating cost per bay $= £6{\cdot}40$ per hour of overtime
Cost of lorry time $= £5$ per hour

Operating with two delivery bays

Estimated daily cost = day-time operating cost + overtime operating cost
$$+ \text{charge for lorry time}$$

$$= 2 \times 8 \times 5 + \frac{8{\cdot}08}{2} \times 6{\cdot}40 + \frac{4585}{2} \times \frac{5}{60}$$

$$= 80 + 25{\cdot}86 + 191{\cdot}04$$

$$= £296{\cdot}90$$

Operating with three delivery bays

Estimated daily cost = day-time operating cost + overtime operating cost
$$+ \text{charge for lorry time} + \text{cost of new bay}$$

$$= 3 \times 8 \times 5 + \frac{2{\cdot}83}{2} \times 6{\cdot}40 + \frac{2690}{2} \times \frac{5}{60} + 12$$

$$= 120 + 9{\cdot}06 + 112{\cdot}08 + 12$$

$$= £253{\cdot}14$$

It therefore appears that construction of a third delivery bay will produce a substantial reduction in costs. However, this conclusion is based on simulation of just two days. Before taking a decision the simulations should be extended over a much longer period. We should also check that the simulation results are realistic by comparing the results of the two bay simulation with the results obtained in practice. The average daily overtime worked and the average waiting time per lorry should be comparable. If they are not, then the simulation model must be modified to bring it closer to the real-life system.

Something else which we should consider is whether there are other alternatives which will give an even lower daily cost than the three delivery bays. Possibly construction of a fourth delivery bay, if there is space available, will reduce costs even further. Another possibility is that, instead of constructing extra delivery bays, money should be spent on reducing unloading time per lorry either by greater mechanisation or by increasing the number of men in each unloading gang. Each of these alternatives could be readily evaluated by simulation.

Varying arrival rates

In the previous example it is unlikely that the pattern of arrivals will remain

Table 5.7
Simulation of two days' operations with 2 and 3 delivery bays

Random number	Time between lorry arrivals (min.)	Lorry arrival time	2 delivery bays				3 delivery bays			
			Bay no.	Unload start time	Unload finish time	Total lorry duration	Bay no.	Unload start time	Unload finish time	Total lorry duration
Day 1										
41	15	08·15	1	08·15	09·15	60	1	08·15	09·15	60
34	15	08·30	2	08·30	09·30	60	2	08·30	09·30	60
20	5	08·35	1	09·15	10·30*	115	3	08·35	09·35	60
78	45	09·20	2	09·30	10·45*	85	1	09·20	10·35*	75
16	5	09·25	1	10·30	11·30	125	2	09·30	10·45*	80
80	55	10·20	2	10·45	11·45	85	3	10·20	11·20	60
46	25	10·45	1	11·30	13·30*	165	1	10·45	11·45	60
07	5	10·50	2	11·45	13·45*	175	2	10·50	11·50	60
24	5	10·55	1	13·30	14·30	215	3	11·20	13·20*	145
26	15	11·10	2	13·45	14·45	215	1	11·45	13·45*	155
91	75	12·25	1	14·30	15·45*	200	2	13·00	14·00	95
26	15	12·40	2	14·45	16·00*	200	3	13·20	14·20	100
39	15	12·55	1	15·45	16·45	230	1	13·45	14·45	110
08	5	13·00	2	16·00	17·00	240	2	14·00	15·00	120
96	95	14·35	1	16·45	17·45	190	3	14·35	15·50*	75
33	15	14·50	2	17·00	18·00	190	1	14·50	16·05*	75
06	5	14·55	1	17·45	18·45	230	2	15·15	16·15	80
96	95	16·30	2	18·00	19·00	150	3	16·30	17·30	60
40	15	16·45	1	18·45	19·45	180	1	16·45	17·45	60
78	45	No lorry arrivals after 17.00 hours								
Day 2										
14	5	08·05	1	08·05	09·05	60	1	08·05	09·05	60
80	55	09·00	2	09·00	10·00	60	2	09·00	10·00	60
04	5	09·05	1	09·05	10·20*	75	3	09·05	10·20*	75
98	105	10·50	2	10·50	11·50	60	1	10·50	11·50	60
20	5	10·55	1	10·55	11·55	60	2	10·55	11·55	60
58	25	11·20	2	11·50	13·50*	150	3	11·20	13·20*	120
88	65	12·25	1	13·00	14·00	95	1	13·00	14·00	95
83	55	13·20	2	13·50	14·50	90	2	13·20	14·20	60
58	25	13·45	1	14·00	15·00	75	3	13·45	14·45	60
60	25	14·10	2	14·50	16·05*	115	1	14·10	15·25*	75
63	35	14·45	1	15·15	16·15	90	2	14·45	16·00*	75
79	45	15·30	2	16·05	17·05	95	3	15·30	16·30	60
10	5	15·35	1	16·15	17·15	100	1	15·35	16·35	60
52	25	16·00	2	17·05	18·05	125	2	16·00	17·00	60
79	45	16·45	1	17·15	18·15	90	3	16·45	17·45	60
12	5	16·50	2	18·05	19·05	135	1	16·50	17·50	60
73	45	No lorry arrivals after 17.00 hours								

* Unloading time includes a meal break or tea break.

the same over the whole working day. There might be a rush of vehicles in the first and last hours of the working day with a lower arrival rate for the rest of the day. If this is the case, then three distributions of vehicle inter-arrival times will be needed, one for the first hour, one for the middle period and one for the last hour. During the simulation, sampling of vehicle inter-arrival times would be from the first distribution for the first hour of each working day. Then sampling would be from the second distribution and, for the final hour of each working day, sampling would be from the third distribution.

Uses of simulation

Having discussed two examples of the use of simulation we can now summarise the various uses of simulation.

Determination of correct staffing in queueing situations

A queueing situation is one in which a number of customers, who may be people or objects, queue up to be served by one or more servers. The repair of machine breakdowns in a factory is a queueing situation where the customers are machines requiring repair and the servers are breakdown men. In such situations the costs incurred include the cost of customer waiting time and the cost of providing the servers. The aim is usually to determine the number of servers which will minimise the sum of these two costs.

Although analytical solutions are available for very simple cases, most real situations are too complex to be solved analytically. Usually simulation is used instead. By carrying out several simulation runs, each with a different number of servers, total costs can be compared and the staffing level which minimises total costs can be determined.

Determination of the correct number of facilities in complex situations

This is another kind of queueing situation, one where the items providing the service are pieces of equipment instead of people. The delivery bay example was a problem of this type. The customers were lorries and the items providing the service were the delivery bays.

A more complex example would be the operation of a port. The arrival of ships will depend on the tides and the availability of tugs to manoeuvre the ships into a berth. The time to unload and load the ship and the handling equipment required will depend on the type of cargo. Here we

Table 5.8
Random number table

26471	93450	52161	12176	83914	22536	00804	92941	48080	81363
32807	14618	33874	20382	40799	42629	88775	39255	43421	91402
80903	04379	78534	81582	28934	62008	48939	76198	17355	08460
18204	27247	72692	96766	53295	39947	46712	00048	22757	09050
20775	61633	58516	29785	88807	43602	72720	46215	53170	97628
75001	28360	81675	04405	98721	34867	79813	07998	04950	54978
29213	88865	32929	23545	17295	19304	65772	02843	30665	45066
80144	24926	78705	36893	48681	88282	56892	55732	63890	02540
38474	75363	52286	74961	03252	06204	47512	32492	22222	64035
91991	73102	16835	27400	30268	40177	11599	27420	79582	13704
98809	13790	18432	12003	34126	40688	89834	97761	81764	16363
71341	82105	28044	60137	86056	20480	82052	10592	22582	94068
82157	28662	32782	70504	27317	39410	75993	37643	50671	56223
78466	04122	57932	31174	76804	60647	43043	75314	14125	94199
06147	92631	57719	54783	88238	73142	06926	55884	46631	76896
60013	19155	77749	88547	08775	42836	24719	26410	29624	95190
73331	09568	39913	24440	58570	90916	88245	79255	05214	11814
47511	33526	16156	20427	79421	09198	31516	97481	39261	90889
69401	33190	89641	26064	79875	99111	91973	04503	17931	58661
44433	10815	62146	60065	35164	43749	95012	55470	79455	96500
64143	89984	09659	88622	43095	04388	06593	52722	10534	95265
81176	53961	66523	76330	35049	51855	04670	85424	48928	88660
58872	75179	67422	01268	43435	49070	29210	49890	05293	56305
70895	57290	07087	18369	13997	52316	59860	17904	23132	11478
24101	90517	04537	93219	97910	71809	15372	52339	11014	37705
39944	47211	43391	83728	39422	02047	87267	86690	80790	49456
71701	92563	76771	28159	65051	74264	67703	35888	84534	03113
26684	30340	14151	77720	54959	71929	67224	54035	36293	02077
01787	20324	19072	50810	11089	60819	94895	67398	07459	51783
42394	67789	18274	33756	05045	92593	12792	03713	71705	69633
78953	70903	28645	72931	66378	20106	51806	77507	21877	26057
08046	94379	23621	62802	34116	66672	45315	51718	62132	70321
61580	91967	60264	48979	15797	17064	57423	53278	68814	21512
20680	01529	47261	00914	54163	21623	10224	49657	88195	12521
53031	59701	27415	41305	66896	64308	26629	69520	73169	70438
63155	02563	50949	23569	74388	55870	76810	48688	29366	31648
95375	11205	03056	99908	39512	41534	22133	77540	19992	67106
50990	99187	95598	99544	86734	73666	65743	92762	31913	19689
65499	99743	13743	74623	20634	31726	18508	70052	58097	03581
10083	67890	98479	25807	01011	50782	48072	09902	45203	60544
09217	41936	84834	20807	78471	28241	42911	72827	41023	98044
79021	85024	36906	91146	23393	15740	59452	70286	20144	91869
60198	25422	82532	20940	27883	84204	90473	59179	09414	91906
29768	09290	42162	12378	72011	10092	73371	79879	63309	11687
85428	45955	90756	29928	45740	64910	95441	73917	99974	61857

are concerned with a number of interacting facilities, tugs, berths, cranes, etc. Any change in one facility will affect the usage of the other facilities. In order to determine the correct number of tugs a number of simulations could be run, just varying the number of tugs available and keeping everything else constant. Usually we shall be interested in the mix of all facilities which will provide the required service at minimum cost. In order to determine this a very large number of simulation runs must be carried out, varying the numbers of the various facilities until a minimum cost solution is reached.

Analysis of the internal workings of a dynamic system

Frequently a simulation model is constructed, not to solve a specific problem, but to gain a better understanding of the way the system operates. By developing a simulation model of the flow of material and finished goods through a whole company it is then possible to use simulation to investigate the way the company would react to a sudden increase in demand or a strike at a major supplier.

Comparison of alternative investment projects

The return from a given project will depend on a number of uncertain factors which include costs, project life and annual revenue. If probability distributions for each of these variables are constructed, a set of annual cash flows over the life of the project can be obtained by sampling once from each distribution. These cash flows can then be converted to a single return on investment figure. If the exercise is repeated a large number of times then the probability distribution of the return on investment for the project can be built up. In the same way probability distributions of return on investment for alternative projects can be prepared. The distributions can then be compared and the project best meeting the organisation's requirements selected. This approach is called risk simulation.

Economic forecasting

A number of simulation models of national economies have been developed. By simulating the future behaviour of the economy they can be used for short-term forecasting of growth rates, levels of investment, etc. Such models can also be used to evaluate the effects of proposed changes in government policy, for example, a change in the level of income tax.

Training of staff can be accelerated by presenting trainees with a situation requiring a decision and then simulating the effects of the decision taken. In the chemical industry many processes require precise control of temperature, pressure and material addition rates. If training of process operators is carried out on the job there is a high cost in rejected batches and low yields. An alternative is to simulate on a computer the progress of the reactions being controlled. The trainee is given a steady stream of data via a computer terminal and when he wishes to make any adjustments to a process he types the desired adjustment on the terminal keyboard. Each adjustment made is incorporated into the simulation and affects the results being fed to him. The trainee very quickly becomes aware of the size of adjustment necessary to produce a given change in the process and becomes adept at allowing for the time-lag between making an adjustment and the corresponding change in the process occurring. Simulation can also be used to expose the trainee to crisis conditions which may occur infrequently in the real system but where a rapid and correct response is vital.

A special case of the use of simulation in staff training is the business game. A number of competing teams each represent a different company. Each team takes decisions about their company's pricing policy, advertising budget, etc. Simulation is then used to determine the net effect of the decisions made by the various teams. The results are fed back to the teams who then make a further set of decisions, taking into account the new information, and so on. By letting managers see the effects of their decisions almost immediately it is possible to improve their decision making ability significantly.

Advantages and disadvantages of simulation

When trying to decide whether simulation should be used it is usually necessary to compare the use of simulation with two other alternatives.

1 Reaching a decision without further analysis.
2 Constructing a quantitative model of the system and then obtaining an analytical solution to the problem.

Taking the first of these, there are many situations where the best decision is so obvious that the use of simulation is unnecessary. In other situations where the best decision is less clear, simulation will be used provided it is believed that simulation will increase the chances of reaching the best decision and provided the cost of carrying out the simulation is less than the expected benefits.

In those cases where there is a choice between using simulation and obtaining an analytical solution the advantages and disadvantages are summarised below.

Advantages of simulation

1   Simulation can be used to solve problems which are not soluble analytically.

2   It is easier for a manager to understand the output of a simulation, as he can more readily relate it to the real system. He is therefore more likely to accept a simulation-derived solution than an analytically derived solution. In some cases simulation has been used in order to demonstrate to the managers concerned that an analytically derived solution is in fact workable.

3   To obtain an analytical solution a number of assumptions must be made. This is less necessary with simulation. Simulation is sometimes used after a solution has been derived analytically in order to check that the assumptions made in the analytical solution are reasonably valid.

Disadvantages of simulation

1   Solution of a problem by simulation requires a considerable amount of computation. For example, in the simulation of a department of automatic machines, output will be affected by the number of machines, the number of machine minders and the number of breakdown fitters available. We might wish to simulate the effects of each of the following possibilities,

number of machines   20, 21, 22, 23, 24
number of machine-minders   4, 5, 6
number of breakdown fitters   1, 2, 3

This gives a total of forty-five separate simulation runs which might need to be carried out.

2   The results obtained from a particular simulation run are estimates subject to statistical error. Therefore any conclusions we draw about the relative merits of alternative operating policies will also be subject to error. By increasing the length of each simulation run the statistical error can be made arbitrarily small but this will considerably increase the amount of computation necessary.

3   Simulation is non-optimising. The user will of course carry out several simulation runs, each one simulating a different operating policy, and will then select the policy giving the best results. However, there is no guarantee that his set of operating policies will include the optimal operating policy.

Consider the following situation where we wish to select the value of variable x which minimises total annual costs. Suppose that the cost curve is as shown in Figure 5.1.

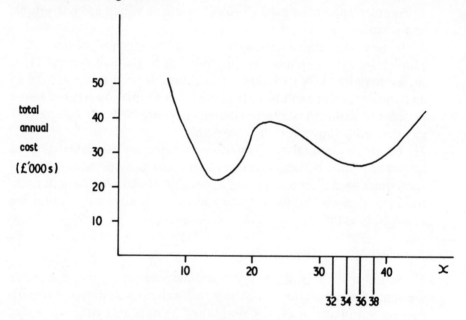

Fig. 5.1   Simulation using the values of x shown indicates an apparent minimum at x = 34

Initially we carry out simulation runs for x = 10, 20, 30, 40.

x	Total annual cost (£)
10	36,000
20	36,000
30	30,000
40	30,000

The minimum would seem to lie between x = 30 and x = 40, so we carry out further simulation runs at x = 32, 34, 36, 38.

x	Total annual cost (£)
32	28,000
34	26,300
36	26,500
38	27,600

We therefore select $x = 34$ as the optimal solution, but this is in fact a local optimum, the true optimum lying at $x = 14.5$.

It is of course fairly unusual to get a cost curve of the shape shown and so local optimisation does not usually arise. However, it is important in simulation that all reasonable alternatives are considered.

The structure of a simulation

In formulating a simulation model an important consideration is how the simulation will be made to progress through time. This is particularly important for computer simulation models as the time flow mechanism must be built into the computer program.

There are two general types of time mechanism,

Fixed time increments – the system is updated by uniform increments of time

Variable time increments – the system is updated to the time when the next event is due to take place

Fixed time increments

This is the method which was used in the stock control simulation example. Although we can expect changes in stock level to be taking place throughout the working day, our simulation only updates the changes in stock level once a day. So in this case the fixed time increment is one working day.

In general, the fixed time increment can be any uniform interval of time, e.g. 10 seconds, 1 hour, 3 months. Each time the simulation is advanced to the next point in time all changes which have occurred since the last update are recorded. After all such changes have been recorded the simulation time is advanced again.

In computer simulation a 'clock' is set up which indicates the point in time which the simulation has reached. The clock is updated in uniform time intervals and each time it is updated the system is scanned to see whether any change has taken place since the previous update. After all such changes have been carried out the clock time is advanced again, and so on.

This type of time mechanism is very easy to program for the computer, but it becomes very inefficient if there are many time periods when no changes take place in the system. For example, this method would have been very inefficient for the stock control example if demand for item WXA231–C had been very low, as on most days there would then be no change in the system.

Variable time increments

This is the method which was used in the loading bays simulation example. At any point in the simulation we know the time when the next lorry will arrive and for each lorry being unloaded we know the time when unloading will be completed. When we wish to advance the simulation time we just check which event is due to occur next and advance to that time. Any changes in the system which occur at that time are carried out and then the simulation time is advanced to the next event time.

In order to use the variable time increment method on the computer each relevant entity in the simulation has a 'clock' associated with it, showing the time when the next event will occur for that entity. In the loading bay example the relevant entities are the lorries. When an event has been completed all the entity clocks are scanned and the simulation clock is advanced to the time at which the next event is due to take place. All the changes in the system resulting from that event are carried out and then the process is repeated.

This method is more difficult to program than fixed time increments, but it is much more efficient when there are long periods between events. Also this method allows time increments to be continuous variables instead of being restricted to multiples of the fixed time increment.

Consider an operator controlling two machines which require attention at random intervals. A bar chart of the operation of the machine is shown in Figure 5.2. Here, although it is possible to use fixed time increments of, say, one minute, it would be inefficient as there are long periods when there are no changes in the system. Also there is the difficulty that run times and load times might not be a whole number of minutes, so that one minute increments might reduce accuracy. For these reasons variable time increments would be used.

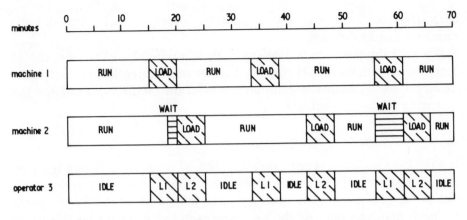

Fig. 5.2   Operation of two machines controlled by one operator

Simulation by computer

Much useful work can be done manually on simulation of relatively simple systems. Manual simulation is also useful in preliminary debugging of more complex simulation models. However, to achieve worthwhile results demands the expenditure of considerable time and the process is extremely tedious. Thus, for most problems simulation by computer is necessary.

While the time to carry out a simulation run on the computer is considerably less than the time to do the same simulation run manually, there is the problem of translating the computer model into a workable computer program. There are four broad approaches to carrying out simulation on a computer.

1   Package programs

If the model is fairly simple and is a common application of simulation a package program may be available which enables the simulation of any system falling into that class to be carried out. Areas for which such programs are available include stock control, one man controlling several machines, and operation of loading bays. To use such a program all the user has to do is to input certain specified information and then run the program.

For a stock control simulation the user might be required to feed in for each stock item the re-order level, the re-order quantity, the distribution of demand for the item and the period to be simulated. After the completion of the simulation run the computer would print out for each item the frequency of stockouts, the average stock level and the number of orders placed.

If a package program is available, this is a relatively cheap method of carrying out simulation. However, the user must carefully check that the assumptions made in the computer simulation model are valid for the system he wishes to simulate.

2 General purpose computer languages

If a package program is not available, then a computer program must be specially written. If the simulation model is only to be used infrequently one of the general purpose languages like BASIC or FORTRAN should be used. Also this may be the best approach for anyone who is already familiar with one of these computer languages and who only rarely becomes involved in simulation.

However, there is a major drawback. The programmer has to write, from scratch, subroutines which are common to almost all simulations. There is also the problem of sequencing events in their proper order and keeping track of simulated time within the computer. This makes programming of even fairly simple simulation models very time-consuming.

3 Simulation languages

Several computer languages have been developed for the specific purpose of easing the programming task of building a simulation model. Most of the commonly recurring tasks of simulation are built into these languages so that it is not necessary to program the tasks in detail. Such facilities include generation of random numbers, sampling from distributions, tabulation of results, etc. These languages also control sequencing of events and keep track of the passage of time during the simulation.

The features of three commonly used simulation languages are outlined below.

ECSL This is a FORTRAN-based language. It is a further development of an earlier simulation language called CSL. It is very powerful and very flexible; FORTRAN statements of subprograms can be included if required. Virtually any simulation model can be programmed using ECSL and a skilful user of ECSL can produce programs which are very efficient from an execution point of view. However, the language is relatively complicated and it takes some time to become familiar with it.

SIMON This is simply a collection of subroutines written either in

FORTRAN or in ALGOL. The user writes his simulation in one of these two general purpose languages, making frequent use of the subroutines. Each subroutine, however, has to be called as needed and there are restrictions imposed by the general purpose language itself on the form of the statements. This means that the language is slightly awkward to use until its intricacies have been mastered. On the other hand, the fact that it is programmed in two of the major general purpose languages means that SIMON is very widely available.

HOCUS   This was developed with the aims of simplicity and ease of use by non-experts. Each entity in the system is conceived of as travelling in a closed loop, alternately through activities and queues. For each activity the user must specify the conditions necessary for the activity to start, the length of time it takes and so on. Each queue simply has a maximum size and a discipline specified.

The language is designed in such a way that hand simulations, using counters, can easily be performed; this is a great aid to debugging.

Although the structure imposed by this language is very restricted, a large number of systems can be formulated in these simple terms. However, there are fairly severe constraints on the complexity of the logic that can be incorporated. Also HOCUS is fairly inefficient in computer running time.

4   Program generators

The main advantage of HOCUS is that the user only has to decide the structure of his simulation. Once this information is input the rest of the work is done by the computer. Most other computer simulation languages require the user to convert his simulation model into a computer program written in the appropriate language. Although this usually produces more efficient programs than with HOCUS, the user does have to spend rather longer learning the language and gaining experience in its use.

However, recently a number of program generators have been developed. Using a computer terminal the user describes the model he wishes to simulate in response to a series of questions from the computer. The computer then generates a computer program to carry out the required simulation, the program being written in a specified simulation language. This simplifies the work of the user considerably while still retaining the efficiency of the chosen language. Once the program has been generated it can either be run immediately using the computer terminal or it can be transferred to a batch computer.

The program generated may well be more efficient than a program written by the user and it will be error-free, so that debugging will not be necessary. In the UK a number of program generators are available; they include SSSS, written by Hugh Lafferty at Sheffield, which produces CSL; interactive ECSL, which is available from Dr. A.T. Clementson at Birmingham and produces ECSL; and DRAFT, written by Stephen Mathewson at Imperial College, which produces SIMON.

An excerpt from a typical run using interactive ECSL is shown below. It is based on the system shown in Figure 5.3.

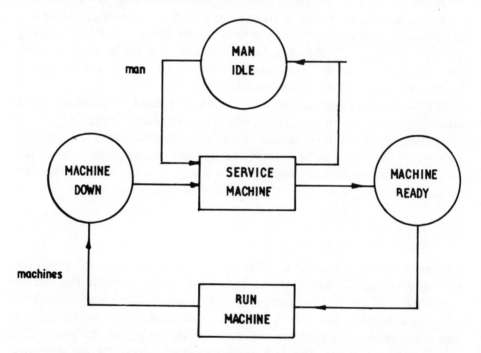

Fig. 5.3   Activity diagram of one man controlling three machines

Excerpt from computer run using interactive ECSL

TYPE NAME OF ENTITIES←MACHINE
HOW MANY?←3
TYPE A LIST OF THE STATES THROUGH WHICH THESE ENTITIES PASS.
THIS SHOULD CONSIST OF EITHER –
      A) AN ALTERNATION OF QUEUES AND ACTIVITIES
           STARTING AND ENDING WITH A QUEUE

OR   B), A LIST OF ACTIVITIES ALONE
              INDICATING THAT THEY CAN OCCUR IN ANY
              ORDER
PRECEDE QUEUES BY Q AND ACTIVITIES BY A
←QDOWN
←ASERVE
←QREADY
←ARUN
←QDOWN
←
―――――

IS THIS CYCLE CORRECT? – YES

Validating the model

The process of building up a simulation model involves formulating a set of relationships between the variables included in the model. It is necessary, therefore, to test that sufficient variables have been included and that the relationships which have been assumed are correct.

This is done by running the simulation under existing conditions and comparing the simulation results with the results obtained in practice. In the delivery bay problem the simulation would first be run with two bays. Then the mean, standard deviation and probability distribution of both lorry waiting time and bay idle time for the simulation would be compared with the corresponding data for the real system.

It is frequently the case that, in an initial formulation of a complex system, variables which are in fact highly relevant to the problem under study are omitted in order to simplify the simulation. The net result may be that the model is too inaccurate to be of any use and must be modified by introducing additional variables.

As costs tend to increase rapidly as the number of variables is increased, it is usual to start with a very simple model and build in more and more detail until the results of the simulation are acceptably close to reality.

Design of simulation experiments

After constructing a simulation model the system then has to be simulated under a variety of conditions in order to determine optimum operating policies. As this may involve a very large number of separate simulation runs it is important to design the experiment so that a minimum of computer time is expended in collecting sufficient information to reach a decision.

Points to be considered are,

(a) starting conditions for the simulation;
(b) the length of each run;
(c) the number of runs under the same conditions;
(d) which variables to measure and how to measure them.

We have already discussed the importance of selecting realistic starting conditions in obtaining efficient simulation runs. Ideally starting conditions derived from the real system should be used. Sometimes this is not possible and there is then the problem of deciding how much of the initial part of the simulation should be discarded as unrepresentative.

In simulation we are usually concerned with obtaining estimates of average queue length, average stock level, etc. The accuracy of these estimates can be improved either by increasing the length of the simulation period or by increasing the number of simulation runs under the same conditions. It is possible to calculate statistically the number of observations necessary to obtain estimates which are within specified limits of accuracy. Another approach is to check the values of the parameters being measured at intervals during each simulation run, stopping when successive checks yield values which are acceptably close together.

In simple problems we are concerned with determining optimal values for one or two variables only. The results of simulation runs under different conditions can then be compared using fairly simple statistical significance tests. However, when there are a large number of variables under consideration, each with a number of alternative values, then evaluation becomes more complex, requiring the use of multivariate analysis techniques.

Applications of simulation

The examples of simulation in this chapter have been considerably simplified in order to illustrate the basic principles of the technique. Simulation has been used to assist in the solution of a wide range of much more complex management problems. The range of applications runs from simulation of the operation of a single section or department through to simulation models of a whole company or industry. It is only possible to mention briefly three examples here. Readers who require more information on applications can make use of the references at the end of this chapter.

Shycon and Maffei have described how the H.J. Heinz Company constructed a major simulation model of their distribution system. Simulation was used to determine the effect on costs of operating with a variety of warehouse configurations. This enabled management to determine the number and approximate locations of warehouses which would give the lowest total distribution costs.

In another application, described by Martin, simulation was used to compare three alternative reservoir schemes. The investigators needed to answer three questions for each of the schemes under consideration.

    1   What will the average daily water yield be?

    2   How will the scheme cope with periods of very high and very low rainfall?

    3   What will the capital and operating costs be?

To make sure that the systems were evaluated over a wide range of operating conditions, each simulation was run for a 100 year time period. The best alternative was then selected by comparing total costs, average yield and the probability of the reservoir level falling outside defined limits.

Probably the most ambitious simulation model constructed so far is the world model developed by Meadows. This model incorporates the inter-relationships between world population, availability of food, consumption of raw materials, pollution, etc. Simulation using this model indicates that, in a relatively short period of time, growth in consumption will outstrip available supplies, leading to widespread shortages. If these predictions are even approximately correct, then there are far-reaching implications regarding our attitude to growth. There has, in fact, been considerable argument about the validity of the model and the assumptions made, but it is a useful first step. Improved versions of the original model have already been constructed and it seems likely that, in the future, simulation will be a major tool of large scale economic planning.

Conclusions

Simulation is a very powerful method of solving management problems. It can be used to select the best of a series of alternatives, to gain a deeper understanding of the behaviour of a complex system, or to determine the overall effects of a proposed change in policy.

Simulation models of very complex systems can be constructed fairly easily. However, the calculations involved in carrying out the simulation are rather tedious, so that use of a computer is almost essential.

The process of applying simulation to a problem can conveniently be summarised as follows:

1 Formulate the problem. This involves discussion with all concerned to determine the objectives of the study and any constraints which must be built into the model.

2 Construct the model. This involves decisions about which parts of the system are to be included in the simulation, which variables are to be measured and what simplifying assumptions can be made.

3 Collect data. This can be quite a lengthy process, since it involves determining the statistical distribution of each variable and the relationships between the variables.

4 Construct a logic diagram and carry out a preliminary hand simulation to test for logical errors.

5 Prepare a computer program if simulation is to be by computer. This will involve the use of a general purpose language such as FORTRAN, or a special simulation language like ECSL.

6 Validate the model. Run the simulation and compare the output with the available data from the real system.

7 Design the experimental runs. This involves deciding initial conditions, run lengths, etc. The application of some thought at this stage can reduce computing time and expense dramatically.

8 Analyse the results, modify the model and repeat the process until acceptable conclusions can be reached.

References

Further reading

Emshoff, J.R. and Sisson, R.L., *The Design and Use of Computer Simulation Models,* Macmillan, 1970.
Jones, G.T., *Simulation and Business Decisions,* Penguin, 1972.
Mize, J.H. and Cox, J.G., *Essentials of Simulation,* Prentice-Hall, 1968.
Naylor, T.H. et al., *Computer Simulation Techniques,* Wiley, 1966.
Schmidt, J.W., *Simulation and Analysis of Industrial Systems,* Irwin, 1970.
Smith, J., *Computer Simulation Models,* Griffin, 1968.
Tocher, K.D., *The Art of Simulation,* Edinburgh University Press, 1963.

Applications

Bisby, H.M.V. and Wharton, F., 'A Computer Model for Freightliner Terminal Management', *International Journal of Physical Distribution,* vol. 5, no. 3, 1975, p. 133.

Lawrence, P.A., 'A Computer Simulation Model for Port Planning', *International Journal of Physical Distribution,* vol. 4, no. 1, 1973, p. 26.

Martin, M.J.C. et al., 'The Evaluation of a Water Resource Project Sponsored by Two Authorities' in *Management Science and Urban Problems,* Saxon House, 1974, p.105.

Meadows, D.L. et al., *The Limits to Growth,* Earth Island Ltd., 1972.

Shycon, H.N. and Maffei, R.B., 'Simulation Tool for Better Distribution' in *New Decision Making Tools for Managers,* Harvard University Press, 1963, p. 224.

Exercises

1   In the stock control example at the beginning of Chapter 5 the works manager has suggested an alternative method of calculating re-order level and re-order quantity. In the case of stock item WXA231–C this would mean

   re-order level   = 60
   re-order quantity = 50

Use the weekly demand figures given in Table 5.1 to simulate the effects of this proposed method. Using the same costs as before estimate the total annual cost of operating the procedure for item WXA231–C and compare it with the two alternatives considered in the text.

2   In the delivery bay example there are other alternatives which have not been considered.

(a)   Construct two additional delivery bays, bringing the total to four. It can be assumed that the depreciation and interest charges for each additional delivery bay will be the same, i.e. £12 per day.

(b)   Continue with the present two delivery bays, but reduce the unloading time per lorry to forty-five minutes by increasing the size of each unloading gang. This will increase the day-time operating cost per bay to £7·50 per hour and the overtime operating cost per bay to £9·50 per hour.

Simulate the effects of each of these alternatives using the sequence of lorry arrival times given in Table 5.7. Estimate the daily cost for each alternative and compare them with the alternatives considered in the text.

3   The maintenance department of a haulage firm has five mechanics available for vehicle servicing. The distribution of number of lorries per day requiring servicing is shown below:

Vehicles requiring servicing	Probability
0	0·02
1	0·07
2	0·15
3	0·19
4	0·20
5	0·16
6	0·10
7	0·06
8	0·03
9	0·01
10	0·01
	1·00

Each vehicle serviced requires one mechanic for a complete working day. Any vehicles which cannot be serviced on a given day are held over until the following day. Simulate the operation of the maintenance department for twenty-five days and calculate the average number of vehicles still requiring servicing at the end of each day and the percentage utilisation of the mechanics.

4   A department contains twelve machines producing identical parts. At present there is an operator for each machine. He is responsible for loading and unloading the machine. Owing to the nature of the material being machined, the process time is highly variable. However, each machine stops automatically when each part is completed.

The distributions of machine running time and servicing time are shown below.

Machine running time (min.)	Freq. (%)	Servicing time (min.)	Freq. (%)
10	10	5	30
15	20	10	40
20	40	15	30
25	20		
30	10		

The works manager is considering increasing the number of machines controlled by each operator.

Simulate production during an eight hour working day for,

(a) 1 operator with 3 machines,

(b) 1 operator with 2 machines.

Material cost = £ 1·00 per part

Labour cost   = £10·00 per operator per day

Overheads   = £10·00 per machine per day

What is the cost per unit produced with

(a) 1 operator controlling 3 machines;

(b) 1 operator controlling 2 machines;

(c) 1 operator controlling 1 machine.

5   Items of a certain type of equipment are shared between several sites and sent out from a central depot to the sites, as required, for varying periods of time. The time taken to complete any one job is measured in multiples of one day.

Tasks which require this particular type of equipment arise in a random fashion on the various sites involved. Demand for units arising in any one day can be based on the following experience of the last 200 days.

Number of new jobs arising in any one day	Frequency of occurrence
0	80
1	74
2	30
3	12
4	4
	200

The jobs take varying times to complete, the completion times being described by the following probability distribution.

Time to complete job (days)	Probability of that time occurring
1	0·190
2	0·160
3	0·120
4	0·100
5	0·085
6	0·065
7	0·055
8	0·045
9	0·034
10	0·030
11	0·024
12	0·019
13	0·016
14	0·012
15	0·010
16	0·008
17	0·007
18	0·006
19	0·005
20	0·004
21	0·003
22	0·002

It can be shown from these distributions that new jobs arise on average at a rate of 0·93 jobs per day and that the average duration time of a job is five days. Therefore, on average, the number of items of this equipment required to be shared between the sites is: $5 \times 0.93 = 4.65$ units.

To provide against occasional heavy demand for this type of equipment, it is proposed to hold a total of six units of this equipment at the depot, to be shared between the sites.

(Assume that the length of time to complete a job includes the time to deliver the equipment from the depot to the site, plus the time to return the equipment to the depot so that it is available for the next job.)

With the given data investigate the likely consequences of the decision to hold six units of this type of equipment. Particularly examine the frequency of occasions when the equipment is under-utilised, as against how frequently and to what extent there may be insufficient units to satisfy demands for this type of equipment.

6   A production centre for the final assembly and testing of gearboxes consists of an assembly line and a test bed with a work in progress area between the assembly line and test bed.

Sets of parts for these gearboxes are delivered to a marshalling area in front of the assembly line, at the beginning of each shift. The number of gearbox parts sets so delivered varies from shift to shift, and is described by the following probability distribution.

Number of gearbox parts sets delivered	Probability
19	0·03
20	0·09
21	0·24
22	0·29
23	0·21
24	0·10
25	0·04

The capacity of the assembly line to assemble parts sets into gearboxes also varies from shift to shift as described by the following probability distribution.

Capacity to assemble	Probability
22	0·10
23	0·26
24	0·31
25	0·21
26	0·10
27	0·02

Gearboxes assembled in one shift are available for testing at the start of the next shift. The test bed has a constant capacity to test twenty-five gearboxes per shift.

Show how you would carry out a Monte Carlo simulation of this process, accumulating data for the average number of units left at the end of each shift in the stores areas and data for the average utilisation of the production and test facilities.

7 A small shop employs two assistants to serve customers.
Time between successive customer arrivals is distributed as follows:

Inter-arrival time (min.)	Cumulative probability
up to 1	0·15
up to 2	0·45
up to 3	0·65
up to 4	0·80
up to 5	0·90
up to 6	0·95
up to 7	0·98
up to 8	0·99
up to 9	1·00

The time taken to serve a customer is as follows:

Service time (min.)	Cumulative probability
up to 2	0·05
up to 4	0·33
up to 6	0·67
up to 8	0·95
up to 10	0·99
up to 12	1·00

Whenever any item falls below a specified level the shelves are replenished from the stockroom. However, the shelves are only replenished when there are no customers waiting to be served.

The time between successive stock items requiring replenishment is distributed as follows:

Time between successive items requiring replenishment (min.)	Cumulative probability
up to 20	0·21
up to 40	0·55
up to 60	0·79
up to 80	0·91
up to 100	0·97
up to 120	1·00

Describe how you would simulate the above system. Carry out a hand simulation of the system for sufficient time to test the correctness of your approach.

8   Imagine that you own a certain petrol station. Describe the data you would collect and the simulation you would carry out in order to determine:
   (a)   How many petrol pumps you should have (assume each one is capable of dispensing all grades of petrol).
   (b)   How many attendants you should employ.

9   A company car park has only one entrance on a busy main road. This means that traffic jams occur as a result of cars trying to enter the car park first thing in the morning. At the moment all employees start at 9.00 a.m. Describe the data you would collect and the simulation you would carry out in order to investigate the effect of changing the working hours so that half the employees start at 8.30 a.m.

Case D   The Northwich Water Undertaking

Introduction

The Northwich Water Undertaking has recently appointed a new Assistant Chief Engineer, Frank Brown. One of his responsibilities is the control of seven service depots. These depots carry out repair and general maintenance of the mains and pipes supplying water, the laying of new mains and the connection of supplies to new consumers.

After a detailed investigation, Mr Brown submitted a report to the Chief Engineer, Charles Warner, recommending that four of the seven service depots should be closed down and that all service work should be carried out from the remaining three service depots.

As this would be a major policy change Mr Warner called a meeting to discuss the report.

Northwich Water Undertaking

The Undertaking is responsible for the distribution of water over an area of 860 square miles. The seven service depots in operation at present are at Northwich, Hanger, Woodford, Stowe, Rayner, Littleham and Penter (see Exhibit 1). Mr Brown has recommended that all servicing should be done from Northwich, Woodford and Stowe.

The workmen are grouped in three-man mainlaying gangs and two-man service gangs as far as possible. Most of the gangs have a small van for travelling between jobs. The vehicles are linked by radio to the parent depot, enabling bursts and other high priority jobs to be attended to with the minimum of delay.

Each depot carries a supply of small spares but larger spares and equipment are kept at the main depot at Northwich and supplied when required.

The meeting

The meeting was attended by the Chief Engineer, the Assistant Chief Engineer, the Chief Accountant and the Operational Research Manager. Mr Brown explained how he had carried out an analysis of journeys between jobs and depots during eight selected weeks. Using costing data supplied by the accounts department he had established that reducing the number of service depots to three would result in a substantial reduction in overhead costs at the expense of a small increase in transport costs.

Mr Brown went on to say that the reduction in depots would increase the time the men spent travelling but that centralisation of the service depots should lead to better co-ordination and improved job allocation. These factors would more than outweigh the effects of the increase in journey time so that the reduced number of depots could be operated with the same number of service men without affecting the service to the public.

After discussion it was generally agreed that there was a financial case to be made for shutting down the four depots. However, the Chief Engineer was very unhappy about the assumption that the number of depots could be reduced without an increase in staff being necessary. He thought that this must lead to an increase in the delay between receiving a job request and carrying out the job.

Mr Brown agreed that the men would spend more time travelling, so that the average time per job would be increased. But he felt that, as the labour utilisation at some of the existing depots was very low, it should be possible to handle the slight increase in work-load without an increase in staff and without an increase in the backlog of jobs waiting for attention.

The Chief Engineer was unconvinced and asked the OR Manager to carry out an independent assessment of the number of men required to operate the proposed system without a reduction in the present level of service provided.

Classification of jobs

As a first step the Operational Research Manager collected from Mr Brown an analysis of the geographic location of jobs visited from depots during the selected eight weeks (Exhibit 2). Then he had an analysis of service jobs carried out. One problem is that different jobs have different priorities. For example, a burst in a 3″ pipe is an emergency requiring immediate attention, while a cracked drain cover can be left unattended for months.

In order to simplify the problem of priority the OR Manager tentatively divided the jobs into groups of roughly similar priority. This gave him the following six classes:

A type jobs:	Bursts in pipes of 3" diameter or more (major failure treated as an emergency).
B type jobs:	Bursts in pipes up to 3" in diameter (moderate loss of water).
C type jobs:	Re-instatement
	Leaking joints
	Repacking valves/glands
	Repairing stop-cocks
	Relaying communication pipes
	Poor pressure
	(slight loss of water or inconvenience to the customer).
D type jobs:	Rebuild stop-cock boxes
	Meter work
	Disconnections
	(unimportant and can remain unattended almost indefinitely).
New services: (NS)	Providing water for building sites Final connections to new buildings.
Mainlaying (ML)	

After a discussion with Mr Brown the OR Manager decided that the order of priority should be:

A
B
C/NS/ML
D

There was another group of jobs involving clearing out the depot yard, tidying up the stores, etc., but these were thought to be time fillers when no other work was available. They were therefore ignored.

Distribution of job times

The OR Manager then asked a member of his staff to carry out an analysis of a sample of job sheets from each depot. For each depot and for each job type the distribution of number of jobs arising per day (Exhibit 3) and the distribution of job times (Exhibit 4) were prepared.

A special problem arose with mainlaying. Whereas all the other job types had durations of, at the most, twenty-one man hours, mainlaying usually involved work for at least one gang for periods varying from a few days to several weeks. For mainlaying, therefore, it was not possible to prepare a distribution of mainlaying job times. Instead the average man hours spent on mainlaying per week was calculated for each depot (Exhibit 5).

Finally the OR Manager drew up the existing organisational structure for the seven depots (Exhibit 6). Having collected all the readily available data, he then had to decide how to use this information to solve his problem.

Assignment

Consider how the OR Manager might proceed and the problems he might encounter.

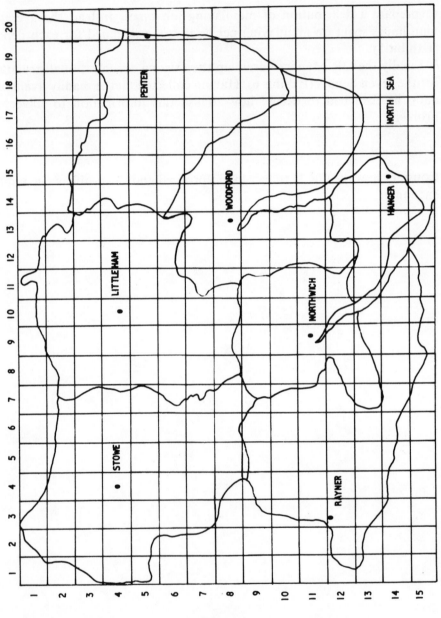

Case D   Exhibit 1   Locations of existing service depots

Exhibit 2

Job locations during the period 1 August 1972–31 July 1973

The table shows the total number of journeys between each grid square and the depots during 8 weeks randomly selected from the above 12 month period.
(Each grid square has dimensions of 2 miles × 2 miles.)

	1	2	3	4	5	6	7	8	9	10	11	12	13	14	15
20					42										
19					104										
18				4		6									
17				2		2			8						
16									9						
15				7	25					7				6	74
14				23	5		16		2				26	16	4
13									288		31	51			
12		5	5	4	16		34		4						
11			20		32			2	2	6	38	98		17	
10		42	82	4						10	36	50		7	
9		26		4	2		9		32	160	190				
8		8				21			6	10					
7				4			16		6					16	
6		10	11				31			12			3	7	
5		2	15			18	5	18					2		
4		18	54		9								5	3	2
3		23	94	36	9	36						52	2		
2		39			18							4			
1															

Exhibit 3

Distribution of jobs arising per day

Job type	Number of jobs	Probabilities						
		Northwich	Woodford	Hanger	Stowe	Littleham	Penter	Rayner
A	0	0·50	0·67	0·79	0·70	0·77	0·78	0·88
	1	0·35	0·27	0·18	0·24	0·20	0·19	0·11
	2	0·12	0·05	0·02	0·04	0·03	0·02	0·01
	3	0·02	0·01	0·01	0·02		0·01	
	4	0·01						
B	0	0·49	0·71	0·81	0·70	0·83	0·82	0·90
	1	0·36	0·24	0·17	0·23	0·15	0·16	0·09
	2	0·13	0·04	0·02	0·05	0·02	0·02	0·01
	3	0·02	0·01		0·02			
	4							
C	0	0·12	0·27	0·49	0·35	0·48	0·46	0·68
	1	0·25	0·35	0·35	0·37	0·36	0·35	0·26
	2	0·27	0·23	0·12	0·19	0·11	0·14	0·05
	3	0·19	0·10	0·03	0·07	0·03	0·03	0·01
	4	0·10	0·03	0·01	0·02	0·02	0·02	
	5	0·04	0·02					
	6	0·02						
	7	0·01						
D	0	0·21	0·41	0·60	0·44	0·62	0·57	0·76
	1	0·33	0·37	0·31	0·35	0·29	0·32	0·21
	2	0·26	0·16	0·08	0·15	0·07	0·09	0·03
	3	0·13	0·05	0·01	0·04	0·02	0·02	
	4	0·05	0·01		0·02			
	5	0·02						
New services	0	0·10	0·26	0·47	0·32	0·48	0·44	0·66
	1	0·23	0·35	0·36	0·36	0·35	0·36	0·28
	2	0·26	0·24	0·14	0·21	0·12	0·15	0·06
	3	0·20	0·10	0·03	0·08	0·03	0·03	
	4	0·12	0·03		0·02	0·02	0·02	
	5	0·06	0·02		0·01			
	6	0·03						

Exhibit 4

Distribution of job times

Job time (man hours)	Probabilities for each job type				
	A	B	C	D	New service
1	–	0·01	0·04	0·08	0·01
2	0·01	0·02	0·11	0·21	0·01
3	0·01	0·06	0·13	0·13	0·02
4	0·01	0·12	0·12	0·10	0·04
5	0·02	0·18	0·11	0·09	0·06
6	0·03	0·14	0·09	0·08	0·10
7	0·06	0·09	0·08	0·07	0·12
8	0·09	0·08	0·07	0·06	0·11
9	0·11	0·06	0·06	0·05	0·10
10	0·13	0·05	0·05	0·04	0·09
11	0·12	0·04	0·03	0·03	0·07
12	0·10	0·03	0·02	0·02	0·06
13	0·08	0·03	0·02	0·02	0·05
14	0·06	0·02	0·02	0·01	0·04
15	0·05	0·02	0·01	0·01	0·03
16	0·04	0·02	0·01	–	0·02
17	0·03	0·01	0·01	–	0·02
18	0·02	0·01	0·01	–	0·02
19	0·02	0·01	0·01	–	0·01
20	0·01	–	–	–	0·01
21	–	–	–	–	0·01

Exhibit 5

Mainlaying

The number of man hours of mainlaying per week tended to be fairly constant for each depot. It was not possible to allocate mainlaying man hours to individual jobs. Mainlaying work at a given location usually continued for several weeks.

Average mainlaying work-load (man hours per week)	
Northwich	285
Woodford	145
Stowe	135
Penter	69
Littleham	97
Hanger	93
Rayner	51

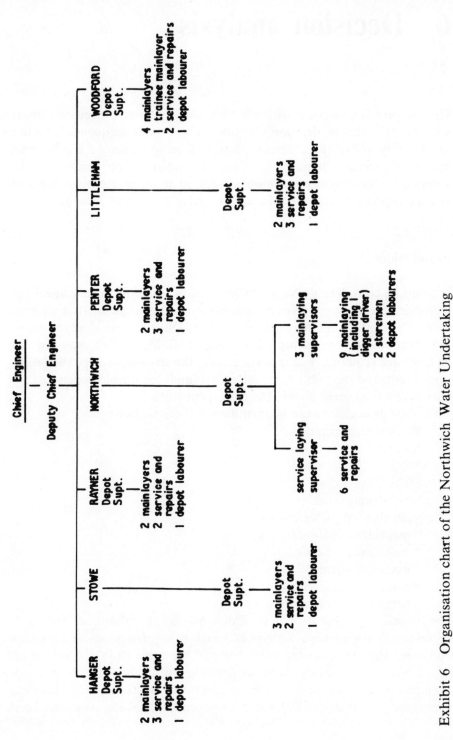

Exhibit 6 Organisation chart of the Northwich Water Undertaking

6   Decision analysis

This chapter is concerned with what are usually termed 'decisions under uncertainty' – that is, decision situations where the consequences of some (or possibly all) of the different courses of action open to the decision maker are uncertain. It presents a systematic and logical procedure whereby a manager can structure a decision situation so as to use his judgement and his experience in a scientific way to arrive at the best decision.

Payoff tables

We start by considering a very simple decision situation. A newsagent has to decide how many copies of a specialist motoring magazine to stock each week. Demand for the magazine fluctuates. During some weeks as many as four could be sold, during others none at all. More often than not two or three are required. The magazine costs the newsagent 40p, the selling price is 60p and the publishers make no refunds for unsold copies.
How many magazines should the newsagent stock?
Five possible decisions can be identified in this situation:
>Stock 0 magazines
>Stock 1 magazine
>Stock 2 magazines
>Stock 3 magazines
>Stock 4 magazines

There are also 5 possible outcomes.
>0 magazines demanded
>1 magazine demanded
>2 magazines demanded
>3 magazines demanded
>4 magazines demanded

The situation is represented in Table 6.1. Each column of the table corresponds to a possible decision and each row corresponds to a possible outcome. The figures in the main body of the table show the profits (£) which result from every possible decision outcome combination. For example, if the newsagent decides to stock two magazines and three are demanded, his costs are £0·80 and his revenue (from the two sales he is able to make) is £1·20 giving a profit of £0·40. If he decides to stock four magazines and two are demanded, his costs are £1·60 and his revenue is £1·20 giving a profit of −£0·40 (i.e. a loss of £0·40).

The numbers in a table such as Table 6.1 are often referred to as payoffs (rather than profits) and the table as a whole is known as a payoff table or payoff matrix.

Table 6.1

Payoff table for magazine example

		Decision: number of magazines stocked				
		0	1	2	3	4
Outcome:	0	0	−0·40	−0·80	−1·20	−1·60
demand for	1	0	0·20	−0·20	−0·60	−1·00
the magazine	2	0	0·20	0·40	0	−0·40
	3	0	0·20	0·40	0·60	0·20
	4	0	0·20	0·40	0·60	0·80

Decision criteria

When outcomes can be predicted with complete certainty, a straight-forward decision criterion such as 'maximise profits', 'minimise costs' or 'maximise net cash flow' is usually sufficient. However, when uncertainty is present, rather more complicated decision criteria are necessary, because usually it is the case that no single decision is best for all outcomes.

Consider the example introduced in the previous section. If the news-agent were a born pessimist he would assume that the worst was going to happen and, each week, choose to stock 0 magazines. On the other hand if he were an optimist by nature he would work on the assumption that the best possible outcome was going to occur and stock four of the magazines.

Already we have formulated two completely different decision criteria. Technically they are known respectively as: *maximin* (short for 'maximise the minimum possible payoff'. i.e. play safe), and *maximax* (short for 'Maximise the maximum possible payoff'. i.e. be optimistic).

Another slightly more complicated decision criterion is known as *minimax regret* – short for 'Minimise the maximum extent to which you may regret that you did not take another decision after the event'. Suppose the newsagent stocks one magazine. If one magazine is required by his customers he will have no regrets. If two magazines are required, we say his regret is £0·20 because he could have made an extra £0·20 by choosing another decision (i.e. he could be £0·20 richer if he had chosen to stock two magazines). If three magazines are required his regret is £0·40 because he could have been £0·40 richer if he had taken another decision (in this case to stock three magazines). If four magazines are required, his regret is £0·60 by the same reasoning. Finally, if 0 magazines are required his regret is £0·40 (he would be £0·40 better off if he had chosen the decision to stock nothing). Table 6.2 summarises the situation.

Table 6.2

Possible regrets if one magazine is stocked

Number required	0	1	2	3	4
Regret if 1 magazine is stocked (£)	0·40	0	0·20	0·40	0·60

The newsagent's maximum possible regret if he stocks one magazine is therefore £0·60. Table 6.3 shows the maximum regret for each of the available decisions. 'Stock one magazine' can be seen from the table to be the best decision under minimax regret (the newsagent is liable to have greater regrets if he takes any other decision).

Table 6.3

Maximum possible regrets for different decisions

Decision: No. of magazines stocked	0	1	2	3	4
Maximum possible regret (£)	0·80	0·60	0·80	1·20	1·60

Expected monetary value

The trouble with the decision criteria mentioned in the previous section is that they do not take any account of how likely the different outcomes are. Maximax, for example, is not a very sensible decision criterion for the newsagent to use if there is a demand for four magazines on only one week in every hundred. On the other hand, if the demand is nearly always for four, then neither maximin nor minimax regret are likely to give very good results.

Thus, although such decision criteria as maximin, maximax and minimax regret can be reasonable, the reader would not be very wise to use them all the time. Indeed, he would find life intolerable if he did so. Maximin, for example, would decree that he must not cross a road for fear of being run over, that he must not eat for fear of being poisoned, etc.

In order to have a rational basis for decision making it is necessary to estimate in some way the probabilities of occurrence of each of the outcomes and then to use these in the decision criterion. Suppose, for example, that the newsagent kept records of the demand for the magazine over a fifty week period as shown in Table 6.4.

Table 6.4

Data on demand for magazine

Demand of magazine	Number of weeks (out of a total of 50) in which demand was observed
0	5
1	10
2	20
3	10
4	5

He could then estimate the probabilities shown in Table 6.5.

Table 6.5

Estimates of probabilities of different demands occurring

Demand for magazine	Probability
0	0·10
1	0·20
2	0·40
3	0·20
4	0·10

This assumes, of course, that the pattern of demand is going to be the same in the future as in the past. One magazine was demanded on ten weeks out of fifty in the past and this leads to a probability of 0·20 for this event happening in the future, etc. If the trading conditions of the newsagent

135

had changed recently adjustments would have to be made to the probabilities.

Now let us consider what the average future profit per week can be expected to be if different decisions are made. Table 6.6 summarises the situation if four magazines are stocked each week.

Table 6.6

Probabilities and profits on the assumption that four magazines are stocked each week

Probability	Profit (£)
0·1	−1·60
0·2	−1·00
0·4	−0·40
0·2	0·20
0·1	0·80

The average profit can be calculated by multiplying probabilities by profits and then adding:

$$\text{Average profit} = 0{\cdot}1 \times (-1{\cdot}60) + 0{\cdot}2 \times (-1{\cdot}00) + 0{\cdot}4 \times (-0{\cdot}40)$$
$$+ 0{\cdot}2 \times 0{\cdot}20 + 0{\cdot}1 \times 0{\cdot}80$$
$$= -0{\cdot}40$$

(The reason why the average profit is calculated in this way can be seen by considering one hundred typical weeks. The profit can be expected to be − £1·60 on ten of the weeks, − £1·00 on twenty of the weeks, − £0.40 on forty of the weeks, £0·20 on twenty of the weeks and £0·80 on ten of the weeks, giving a total profit of £40 over the hundred weeks, i.e. an average profit per week of £0·40.)

Similarly we can write down the average profit per week from other courses of action. 'Stock 3 of the magazines per week' leads to an average profit (£ per week) of:

$$0{\cdot}1 \times (-1{\cdot}20) + 0{\cdot}2 \times (-0{\cdot}60) + 0{\cdot}4 \times 0 + 0{\cdot}2 \times 0{\cdot}60 \times 0{\cdot}1 \times 0{\cdot}60$$
$$= -0{\cdot}06$$

'Stock 2 of the magazines' leads to an average profit (£ per week) of:

$$0{\cdot}1 \times (-0{\cdot}80) + 0{\cdot}2 \times (-0{\cdot}20) + 0{\cdot}4 \times (0{\cdot}40) + 0{\cdot}2 \times (0{\cdot}40 + 0{\cdot}1 \times (0{\cdot}40)$$
$$= 0{\cdot}16$$

'Stock 1 of the magazines' leads to an average profit (£ per week) of:

$$0{\cdot}1 \times (-0{\cdot}40) + 0{\cdot}2 \times 0{\cdot}20 + 0{\cdot}4 \times 0{\cdot}20 + 0{\cdot}2 \times 0{\cdot}20 + 0{\cdot}1 \times 0{\cdot}20$$
$$= 0{\cdot}14$$

Finally the other course of action, of stocking none of the magazines, leads to zero average profit per week. Table 6.7 summarises these results.

Table 6.7

Average profits per week from different decisions

Number of magazines stocked	Average profit (£ per week)
0	0
1	0·14
2	0·16
3	−0·06
4	−0·40

The best decision now clearly emerges as 'stock two magazines each week'. This will give an average profit of £0·16, which is higher than the average profit from taking any other decision.

The average profit which would arise if a certain decision were taken over and over again is known as the expected profit from the decision. (Thus the expected profit from stocking one magazine in any given week is £0·14 etc.) Similarly, average costs are known as expected costs and average net cash flows are known as expected net cash flows, etc.

The general name for the decision criterion used in this section is Maximise Expected Monetary Value (Maximise EMV). If the same decision situation arises over and over again, then use of this criterion will lead to the greatest average profit – or the least average loss – in the long run. As we have seen, the EMV resulting from taking a particular decision is calculated by multiplying the probability of each possible outcome by its payoff and then adding.

One-off decisions

Consider now the following situation:

A certain spare part for a special aircraft costs £1,000 to manufacture if it is manufactured at the same time as the aircraft itself. On the other hand, if a special production run has to be set up after the aircraft has been manufactured, the cost is £8,000 each time the part is produced. (This includes the cost of having the aircraft temporarily grounded.) Past experience with similar aeroplanes leads to 0·3, 0·3, 0·25, 0·1, 0·05 as estimates of the probabilities of 0, 1, 2, 3, or 4 parts respectively being required.

How many parts should be produced?

The probabilities and payoffs are summarised in Table 6.8. (The table shows that, for example, if two spares are produced and three are demanded, the payoff in £'000s is -10 because a cost of £2,000 will be incurred in the initial production and £8,000 will be incurred when a later special production run for one extra spare is carried out etc.)

Table 6.8

Payoffs (£'000s) and probabilities in the aircraft manufacturer example

			Decision: number produced				
		Probability	0	1	2	3	4
	0	0·3	0	−1	−2	−3	−4
	1	0·3	−8	−1	−2	−3	−4
Outcome:	2	0·25	−16	−9	−2	−3	−4
number	3	0·1	−24	−17	−10	−3	−4
demanded	4	0·05	−32	−25	−18	−11	−4

The EMV if 0 are produced
$$= (0 \times 0·3) - (8 \times 0·3) - (16 \times 0·25) - (24 \times 0·1) - (32 \times 0·05) = -10·4$$
Similarly EMV if 1 is produced $\quad = -5·8$
EMV if 2 are produced $= -3·6$
EMV if 3 are produced $= -3·4$
EMV if 4 are produced $= -4·0$

On the basis of the EMV decision criterion it is clear that three spares should be produced. However, the reasons for using EMV are not in this case quite as compelling as they were for the newsagent. His decision was one which was taken regularly every week. Over a long period of time, say, one hundred weeks, the decision with the highest EMV was almost certain to give him the highest profit. In the situation facing the aircraft manufacturer this argument does not apply. We cannot, for example, say that on 30 per cent of the occasions on which the decision is taken 0 spares will be required. The decision is only taken once.

Should EMV be used by a business organisation for one-off decisions? Naturally this depends on the business organisation's attitude to risk. However, a reasonable answer to the question is: yes, providing the sums of money involved are relatively small in relation to the total assets of the organisation. The aircraft manufacturer considered here will presumably be faced with many situations each year which are similar in terms of the sums of money involved to the one above. Providing he always used EMV as his decision criterion in these situations, he should succeed in obtaining good overall results. In fact it can be argued that the net cash flow resulting from the decisions taken by the aircraft manufacturer over a long period of time should roughly equal the sum of the corresponding EMVs. The analogy between the business executive and the bridge player is useful here. A good bridge player (i.e. one who takes good decisions) may do worse than a poor one on a particular hand because of the way the cards happen to lie. In the long run however he will do better.

When relatively large sums of money are involved EMV is not in general an appropriate decision criterion. Consider, for example, a man insuring his house against fire. Suppose that the house is worth £10,000 and has, actuarially speaking, a probability of 0·0001 of being burnt down completely in any one year. (To simplify the situation we suppose that the probability of the house being only partially burnt down is zero.) The man would probably be quite happy to pay a premium of, say £2·50 per annum to insure against fire even though the expected cost to him resulting from fire damage in any one year is only $0·0001 \times £10,000 = £1·00$. The reason is, of course, that £10,000 is a very large sum of money to him. He cannot afford to 'play the averages' and use EMV.

Viewed from the insurance company's point of view, of course, the situation is quite different. £10,000 is not a large sum of money; most of the company's transactions involve risks of paying out tens of thousands of pounds. EMV is a reasonable decision criterion and the company should be perfectly happy to insure the house because its EMV from doing so is positive, i.e. $£2·50 - £1·00 = £1·50$.
(This calculation does, of course, ignore the administrative, overhead and other costs incurred by the insurance company.)

Subjective probabilities

In both of the situations considered so far the decision maker has been able to estimate in some way the probabilities associated with uncertain events. The newsagent was, it will be remembered, able to base his probabilities on the demand data recorded during a fifty week period, and in the aircraft manufacturer's situation we assumed that it was possible to estimate the required probabilities from historical data collected for similar aircraft.

Consider by contrast the following situation:

A large firm has just invented a new product which it is not at present equipped to manufacture itself. It has three choices.

1   Acquire the necessary machinery to carry out the manufacture itself.

2   Sell all rights to the product to another firm.
3   Sell rights on a royalty basis to another firm.

The marketing manager's own instincts tell him that either the product will 'catch on', achieving total sales of 20,000–25,000, or it will 'flop', achieving 2,500–5,000 sales, and on this basis the payoff matrix in Table 6.9 has been drawn up.

Table 6.9

Payoffs (£'000s) in new product example

		Decision		
		Manufacture	Sell all rights	Sell on royalty basis
Outcome:	Catches on	100	10	55
	Flops	−175	10	5

What decision should be taken?

If decision analysis is to be used, the next stage must be to assign probabilities to the two outcomes 'catches on' and 'flops'. As the new product is different from any previously encountered, it is reasonable to assume that there are no data which can be used. It then becomes necessary to rely on what are termed 'subjective probabilities'. These are probabilities which the decision maker himself assesses on the basis of his own skill, knowledge, judgement and experience. To illustrate the basic idea, suppose the marketing manager in the above situation were a betting man. We could ask him: What are the best odds you can give us on the product catching on? He might after some thought say: '3:2 on'. This means that we would have to stake £3 in order to win £2. It would indicate that the marketing manager assessed subjectively the probability of the outcome 'catches on' at 3/5 or 0·6.

If the marketing manager were not familiar with betting odds, an alternative approach would be to compare the unknown subjective probability with different known frequency probabilities by means of questions such as: Imagine a ball being drawn at random from an urn containing fifty red balls and fifty black balls. Which would you rather bet on: the ball being red or the new product catching on?

If the marketing manager preferred to bet on the ball being red the proportion of red balls would be reduced and the question repeated; if not, the proportion would be increased and the question repeated. Eventually the value of the unknown subjective probability would be pinpointed reasonably accurately. (If the marketing manager were a sceptic these questions would at the same time provide a clear demonstration of the fact that subjective probabilities do exist and do have a meaning!)

Suppose that the marketing manager does in fact assess a probability of 0·6 for the product catching on. Then:

1   EMV from decision 'manufacture' is: $(100 \times 0·6) - (175 \times 0·4)$
$= -10$.
2   EMV from decision 'sell all rights' is $+10$.
3   EMV from decision 'Sell on royalty basis' is: $55 \times 0·6 + 5 \times 0·4$
$= 35$.
'Sell on a royalty basis' is therefore the best decision.

Decision trees

Let us now suppose that there is an additional complication in the situation considered in the previous section. Suppose that, if the firm manufactures the product itself and if the product catches on, the firm will then have the opportunity of attempting to develop an improved design for the product. (It need not accept this opportunity.) In the event of the development being a success £150,000 extra profit would be made. If it were a failure £100,000 loss would be incurred.

This cannot be analysed in quite the same way as the other situations considered so far. It is what might be termed technically a 'sequential decision situation'. If one decision is taken, then in certain circumstances the firm has the opportunity to take another decision later. Payoff tables are not sufficient to analyse such situations. It is necessary to use what are termed decision trees. These are diagrams which represent all the different possible sequences of decisions and outcomes that can occur. Figure 6.1 is the decision tree for the situation just described.

It will be noted that there are two sorts of nodes on the tree. The rectangular shaped nodes (■) are known as decision nodes. They represent points in time where a choice has to be made between alternative courses of action. The circular nodes (●) are known as outcome or event nodes. They represent points in time where events outside the control of the decision maker happen.

In Figure 6.1 the first node is a decision node and the branches emanating from the node correspond to the three decisions initially open to the company. The tree shows in a clear way that:

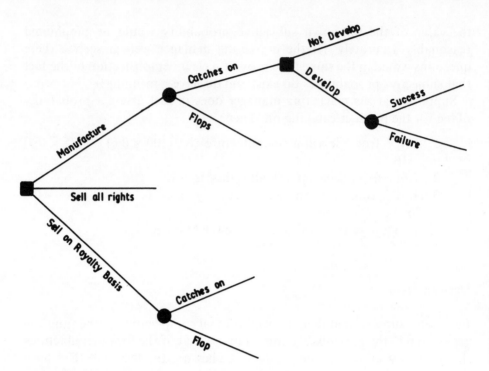

Fig. 6.1   Decision tree for inventor example

1   If the company chooses to sell all rights, no further decisions or events affect its profit.

2   If the company chooses to sell on a royalty basis, just one subsequent event (i.e. whether the product catches on or flops) affects the profit.

3   If the company chooses to manufacture itself, then the first thing that happens is that the product either catches on or flops. If it catches on, the decision on whether to develop a new design is taken. If the firm decides to develop, then the development is either a success or a failure.

In order to analyse a decision tree it is necessary:

1   to put probabilities on the branches emanating from outcome nodes to indicate the chances of the different outcomes occurring.

2   to put payoffs at the ends of the terminal branches to indicate the consequences of the different possible sequences of decisions and outcomes.

This has been done in Figure 6.2. The figure assumes that the marketing manager assesses the probability of the product catching on at 0·6 and the

142

probability of development proving a success at 0·8. Most of the payoffs in the figure can be taken straight from Table 6.9. (For example the table shows that the sequence: 'Sell on a royalty basis', 'Catches on' leads to a payoff (in £'000s) of 55.) Note, however, that the payoff of £250,000 from the sequence 'Manufacture', 'Catches on', 'Develop', 'Success' must be calculated from the information given in this section. It is the sum of £100,000 from the product catching on and £150,000 from successful development. Similarly the payoff of £0 from the sequence 'Manufacture', 'Catches on', 'Develop', 'Failure' must be calculated as £100,000 from the product catching on minus £100,000 from successful development.

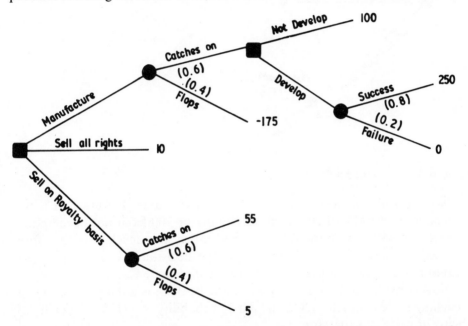

Fig. 6.2 Decision tree with probabilities and payoffs for inventor example

Figure 6.2 is a complete description of the decision situation. Once it has been drawn, a procedure known as roll-back can begin. This is illustrated in Figure 6.3. It involves working from the right of the decision tree to the left asking at each node (decision node or event node) the question 'How much is it worth to be at this node?' One of the first nodes encountered (see Figure 6.3) is the node D. If we are at node D, the tree tells us that there is a 0·8 probability of a payoff of +250 and 0·2 probability of a payoff of 0. The value (assuming EMV) of being at node D is therefore:

$$0·8 \times 250 + 0·2 \times 0 = 200$$

(measured in £'000s). This has been put adjacent to node D in Figure 6.3.

143

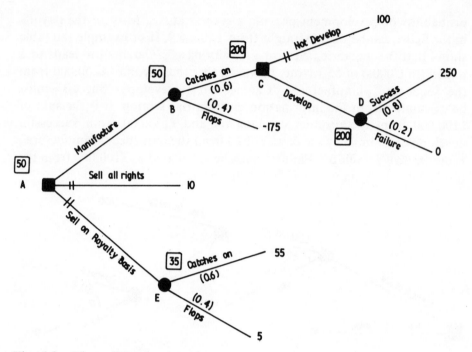

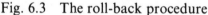

Fig. 6.3   The roll-back procedure

Now consider node C. Node C is a decision node. If we are at it we can choose an EMV of 200 from developing or 100 from not developing. Clearly we will choose the former. The branch 'not develop' is therefore crossed with two lines to indicate that the decision which it represents would not be chosen and 200 is put adjacent to node C.

Now consider node B. If we are at node B, there is a 0·6 probability of reaching node C worth +200, and a 0·4 probability of −175. The value of being at node B is therefore:

$$0·6 \times 200 + 0·4 \times (-175) = 50$$

Finally the value of being at node E is:

$$0·6 \times 55 + 0·4 \times 5 = 35$$

The value of being at node A (i.e. at the beginning of the tree) is therefore +50 and the best initial decision is 'manufacture'. (It is interesting to note from the analysis in the previous section that without the opportunity to develop an improved design the best decision is 'sell on a royalty basis', 'manufacture' being worth only −10.)

To summarise, decision trees are a straightforward way of applying the expected monetary value decision criterion to situations where a number of decisions are made sequentially. The example we have considered has been a very simple one. In most real life situations the decision tree is very much more 'bushy'. It then serves the very important role of breaking down a highly complex problem into a number of simpler ones, providing at the same time a focus for the expert subjective judgements of managers from production, marketing, finance and other functions.

Expected value of perfect information

We now carry the example just considered still further by supposing that the marketing manager has the opportunity to buy market research information. Most information of this kind is of course imperfect; that is, it does not make us completely certain about something we were previously uncertain about. However, it is often useful to suppose that a manager can buy perfect information, i.e. that he can completely resolve an uncertainty in a situation. This is what we do here. We assume that the marketing manager can, at no cost, obtain information which will tell him for certain whether the product will catch on or flop.

The first stage in the analysis is to draw an extra branch on the decision tree (see Figure 6.4). The marketing manager assessed the probability that the product would catch on at 0·6. It follows – and this is the crucial stage in the argument – that this must be his probability that perfect information will tell him that the product will catch on.

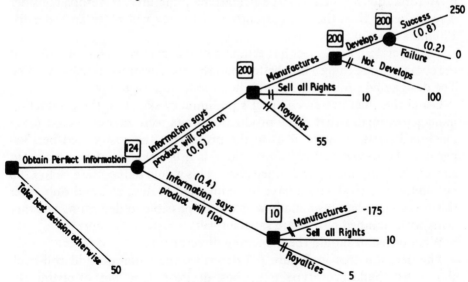

Fig. 6.4   Calculating the value of perfect information

145

Roll-back (see Figure 6.4) shows that the company's EMV in the new situation is 124 (in £'000s). This is considerably more than the company's previous best EMV of 50. The difference between 124 and 50, i.e. 74, is known as the *expected value of perfect information*. It can be interpreted as the maximum price which the company should ever be prepared to pay for market research information. It is the maximum amount by which extra information on the sales of the product can increase the EMV. Therefore, if the information costs more than £74,000, however good it is, it can't be worth it.

This type of analysis is useful in a wide variety of situations. A manager's natural inclination is always to collect as much information as is possible before making any decision. This can be very wasteful if the information is very expensive or if the chance of it causing him to change his decision is very small.

Sensitivity analysis

Once the roll-back analysis has been carried out it can be useful to test how sensitive the final decision is to the different probabilities. Consider the following situation.

The managing director of a firm manufacturing electronic control equipment has been invited to build a prototype of a special control unit used by Aeropa International, a large aircraft manufacturer. If Aeropa consider it to be better than the one currently in use they will place an order for 100 units at £500 each.

The chief design engineer has estimated that there is a 0·6 probability of the company designing a unit better than the one currently used by Aeropa. The design and production would, he estimated, cost £5,000.

Using the chief design engineer's preliminary sketches, the production manager estimates that if the production units were manufactured using machined parts throughout as in the prototype, the cost would be £300 per unit. However, he judges that there is a 0·7 chance of being able to substitute stampings for machined parts. This would reduce the cost to £200 per unit, but £3,000 would have to be invested in dies, etc. and only after this investment had been made would it be possible to determine whether units with stamped parts were satisfactory.

What decision should the managing director take?

The decision tree in Figure 6.5 describes the situation and roll-back shows that 'build prototype' is the best decision. One way of testing the sensitivity of this decision to the probability of 0·6 estimated for Aeropa ordering would involve changing this probability to 0·5 (changing at the same time the probability of Aeropa not ordering to 0·5) and carrying out the roll-back procedure again. If the decision remained unchanged the probability could then be changed to 0·4 etc.

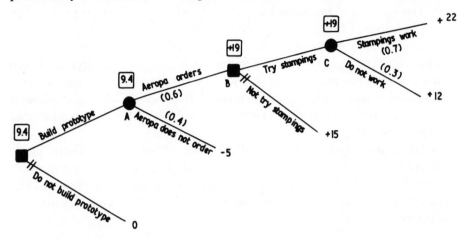

Fig. 6.5   Decision tree for Aeropa International example

A more general procedure is to replace the probability of Aeropa ordering by a variable, say, p, on the tree and the probability of Aeropa not ordering by $1 - p$. Roll-back can then be carried out in terms of p.

The value of being at node B (see Figure 6.5) is $+19$ (regardless of the value of p). The value of being at node A is:

$$19p - 5(1 - p) = 24p - 5$$

'Build prototype' is therefore still the best decision if:

$$24p - 5 > 0$$

i.e. if $24p \quad > 5$

i.e. if $\quad p \quad > 0·208$

The decision is therefore not very sensitive to the probability of Aeropa ordering – in fact we have shown that this probability would have to drop from its present level of 0·6 to almost 0·2 before the decision would be changed.

Before carrying out the above analysis it is usually worth testing whether the decision is at all sensitive to the probability in question. This is done by changing the probability first to 0 and then to 1, observing in each case whether the decision changes. In the case of the probability of Aeropa ordering the units, this analysis would have shown that the decision is at least a little sensitive to the probability of Aeropa ordering (if the probability is set equal to 1 the prototype should be built, if it is put equal to 0, it should not). Consider however the sensitivity of the decision to the probability of being able to substitute stampings for machined parts. If this probability becomes 1, the prototype should, of course, be built. If it becomes 0, then:

The value at C becomes 12

The value at B becomes 15

The value at A becomes $0.6 \times 15 + 0.4 \times 5 = 7$.

'Build prototype' is still the best decision. It is true that the decision taken at node B has changed. However, this is not important; it is the decision initially open to the managing director that concerns us at the moment and we can say that this decision is not at all sensitive to the probability of stampings working.

Sensitivity analyses are especially useful in situations where many different subjective probabilities are involved. They enable the important uncertainties to be separated from the less important ones very quickly, allowing more managerial time to be devoted to a consideration of the former.

Bayesian analysis

We now consider in rather more detail how to deal with a situation where a firm has the option to buy further information (not in this case perfect information) before making a decision.

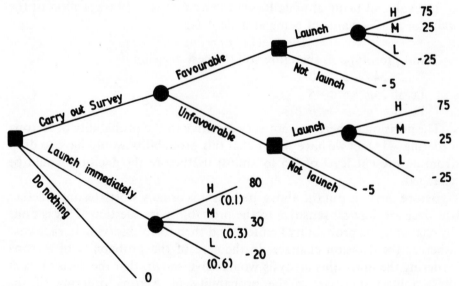

Fig. 6.6 Decision tree for new product launch

The possible sales levels for a new product have been divided into three categories: high (H), medium (M) and low (L). High sales are considered by the marketing manager to have a probability of 0·1 and would lead to a net cash flow (discounted over time) of £80,000. Medium sales have a probability of 0·3 and would lead to a net cash flow of £30,000. Low sales have a probability of 0·6 and would lead to a net cash flow of −£20,000. Before deciding whether to launch the new product the firm can, at a cost of £5,000, carry out a quick market survey which would give either a 'favourable' or an 'unfavourable' result.

Should the survey be carried out? The decision tree is shown in Figure 6.6.

In order to carry out the roll-back analysis it is clear from the figure that we need to know:

(a) the probability of a favourable result from the survey;
(b) the probability of high sales if the survey result is favourable;
(c) the probability of medium sales if the survey result is favourable;
(d) the probability of low sales if the survey result is favourable;
(e) the probability of an unfavourable result from the survey;
(f) the probability of high sales if the survey result is unfavourable;
(g) the probability of medium sales if the survey result is un-favourable;
(h) the probability of low sales if the survey result is unfavourable.

b, c, d, f, g, and h are known as *conditional probabilities*. They are the probabilities of a certain event happening given that another event has already happened. a and e are *unconditional probabilities*.

All eight probabilities could be assessed by the marketing manager and the roll-back analysis could then be carried out. However, there would then be a problem in that the 0·1, 0·3 and 0·6 unconditional probabilities already assessed for high, medium and low sales might not be consistent with these eight probabilities. (As the reader who has studied probability theory will verify:

Prob. of high sales, i.e. 0·1 should equal $a \times b + e \times f$
Prob. of med. sales, i.e. 0·3 should equal $a \times c + e \times g$
Prob. of low sales, i.e. 0·6 should equal $a \times d + e \times h$.

For this reason the next stage is usually to ask the marketing manager to assess three probabilities which can be used in conjunction with the unconditional probabilities of high, medium and low sales in order to arrive at the eight probabilities a to h above. These three probabilities are:

(i) the probability of a favourable result from survey if sales are high;
(ii) the probability of a favourable result from survey if sales are medium;

(iii)   the probability of a favourable result from survey if sales are low.

Let us suppose their values are 0·9, 0·5 and 0·2 respectively. They can be represented together with the 0·1, 0·3 and 0·6 probabilities of H, M and L on a diagram. Figure 6.7 is the first stage in the drawing of the diagram. It shows a square 1, unit by unit divided into 3 rectangles. The left rectangle represents the probability of high sales and has area 0·1. The middle one represents the probability of medium sales and has area 0·3. The right hand one represents the probability of low sales and has area 0·6.

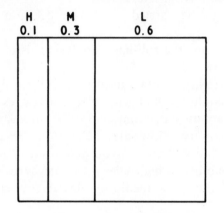

Fig. 6.7   First stage in drawing probability diagram

Each rectangle is then divided into two parts (see Figure 6.8). The shaded part represents a favourable result from the survey and the unshaded part an unfavourable result. We know that if sales are high the probability of a favourable result is 0·9. This means that the shaded area must be nine-tenths of the total area in the left hand rectangle. Similarly it must be half the total area in the middle rectangle and one-fifth of the total area in the left hand rectangle.

Figure 6.8 is therefore a diagrammatic representation of all of the marketing manager's subjective probability assessments. Any of the eight probabilities required for the decision tree can be picked from it.

The probability of a favourable result from the survey is the total shaded area = $0·9 \times 0·1 + 0·5 \times 0·3 + 0·6 \times 0·2$

   = 0·36

The probability of an unfavourable result from the survey is the total unshaded area, i.e. 0·64.

The probability of high sales given a favourable result from the survey is the probability that a point selected at random is in area ABCD if we already know that it is in the shaded area.

150

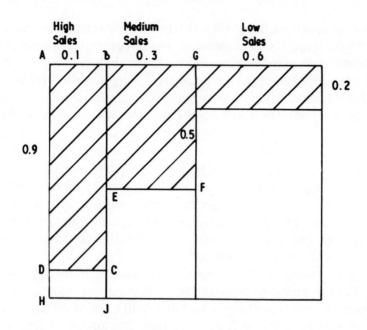

Fig. 6.8 The probability diagram

It is:
$$\frac{\text{Area ABCD}}{\text{Total shaded area}} = \frac{0 \cdot 09}{0 \cdot 36} = \frac{1}{4}$$

Similarly the probability of medium sales given a favourable result from the survey is:
$$\frac{\text{Area BEFG}}{\text{Total shaded area}} = \frac{0 \cdot 5 \times 0 \cdot 3}{0 \cdot 36} = \frac{5}{12}$$

Similarly: Probability of low sales given a favourable result from the survey = 1/3.

Probability of high sales given an unfavourable result from the survey is:
$$\frac{\text{Area CDHJ}}{\text{Total unshaded area}} = \frac{1}{64}$$

Probability of medium sales given an unfavourable result from the survey = 15/64.

Probability of low sales given an unfavourable result from the survey = 3/4.

It is now left to the reader to finish off the analysis by putting the probabilities on Figure 6.6 and carrying out the roll-back procedure. The result he obtains should be:

        EMV of do nothing   : 0
        EMV of launch immediately : 5
        EMV of carry out survey   : 4·3

In this section we have been using a diagrammatic version of what is known as Bayes' theorem. It is, in essence, a way of converting the unconditional probability of an event happening into the probability that it will happen conditional on a survey, experiment etc. giving a certain result. The unconditional probability of an outcome is known as its *prior probability*. The conditional probability is known as the outcome's *posterior probability*.

Utility

Most people when given a choice between £100,000 for certain and £250,000 with probability 0·6 will choose the former, even though it has a smaller EMV. Utility theory – although not widely used in any formal way in business at present – provides a useful conceptual framework for understanding such decisions. It also provides a decision criterion for situations where outcomes are non-monetary.

The theory starts with the basic assumption that the decision maker wishes to take decisions consistently. This means no more than that the decision maker wishes to obey some fairly natural rules such as: If outcome A is preferred to outcome B and outcome B is preferred to outcome C, then outcome A should be preferred to outcome C.

The theory shows that there must be some scale – called the utility scale – on which the value of outcomes can be measured. (This scale may or may not correspond to an ordinary monetary scale, depending on the circumstances.) Once the scale has been determined the decision maker should use *maximise expected utility* as his decision criterion. This means that he should value a decision by multiplying the probability of each possible outcome by its utility and then adding these together. The decision

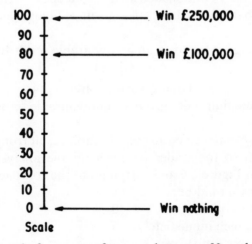

Fig. 6.9   Utility scale for sums of money between £0 and £25,000

criterion is therefore the same as maximise expected monetary value except that monetary value must be replaced by utility in the calculations. If a decision tree is used, it is utilities and not monetary payoffs which must be put at the end of the terminal branches.

Thus an individual's scale of values (i.e. his utility scale) for the outcomes win nothing, win £100,000, win £250,000 might be as shown in Figure 6.9. The utility of 'win £100,000' in Figure 6.9 is 80 and the expected utility from:

0·6 chance to win £250,000
0·4 chance to win nothing $\Big\}$ is 0·6 × 100 + 0·4 × 0 = 60

explaining why the former would be preferred to the latter.

Utilities can also be used for non-monetary outcomes. Figure 6.10 shows what might be an individual's scale of values for the four alternatives: live in London, live in provinces, live abroad but in Europe or N. America, live abroad not in Europe or N. America.

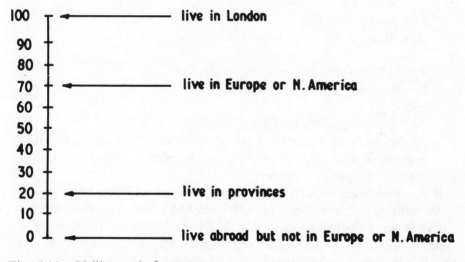

Fig. 6.10   Utility scale for non-monetary outcomes

Suppose the individual is offered two jobs. Job A gives a 50:50 chance of working in London or the provinces. Job B is certain to involve the individual in living abroad: in Europe or N. America with probability 0·7, elsewhere with probability 0·3.

The utility of Job A is: 0·5 × 100 + 0·5 × 20 = 60.

The utility of Job B is: 0·7 × 70 + 0·3 × 0 = 49.

Job A should therefore be chosen.

Two points should be noted about utilities.

1 There is no reason at all why two different people should have the same utility scales. Utilities are very much personal value judgements. (In this respect they are analogous to subjective probabilities.)
2 A utility scale is not fixed until two points on it have been fixed. (In this respect it is like a scale for measuring temperature.) In the above two examples it was assumed that the utility of the best outcome was 100 and that the utility of the worst outcome was 0. This is a sensible convention to adopt.

Finally it is quite instructive to determine your own personal utility scale for sums of money between say £0 and £5,000. The first stage involves interrogating yourself so as to ascertain what a 50:50 gamble on these two sums of money is worth to you. What would you sell such a gamble for? £4,000? Yes, you probably would. £100? Probably not. Eventually you should obtain a sum of money, say £X, which is equivalent to a 50:50 gamble on £0 and £5,000. If:

utility £0 $= 0$
and utility of £5,000 $= 100$
then utility of £X $= 0{\cdot}5 \times 100 + 0{\cdot}5 \times 0$
$= 50$

Similarly the sum of money equivalent to:
(a) a 50:50 gamble on £0 and £X
and
(b) a 50:50 gamble on £X and £5,000
can be obtained. These have utilities of 25 and 75 respectively. Finally a graph of utility against money can be plotted. Figure 6.11 shows some of the possible shapes.

If you have a curve such as curve A in Figure 6.11 you tend to avoid risks, refusing gambles which on a straight EMV basis you should accept. Curve B on the other hand means that you like taking risks, accepting gambles which on an EMV basis are unfair. Curve C is a compromise; you like to gamble where small sums of money are involved but tend to play safe when larger amounts are at stake. Lastly if you have utility curve D it can be said that you faithfully follow the EMV decision criterion in your personal dealings over the range of sums of money considered.

Decision analysis in practice

The decision analysis methodology has now been used in a large number of different business situations (see references). The main advantages and disadvantages of the approach are summarised in Table 6.10.

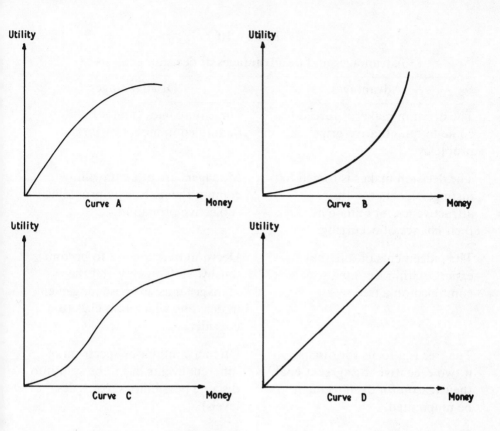

Fig. 6.11   Typical utility curves

The major advantage of decision analysis is undoubtedly the discipline which the decision tree imposes on the manager. It forces him to look ahead, often with the result that he appreciates aspects of his situation which he would not have appreciated otherwise. Sometimes it even happens that completely new courses of action occur to a manager half-way through drawing a tree.

Of the disadvantages, those concerned with the difficulties in quantifying outcomes and obtaining subjective probabilities are probably the most serious. However, it should be noted that, even when none of the outcomes can be quantified and even when no subjective probabilities are forthcoming, it is possible to draw the tree and to use it as a means for displaying the different possible consequences of different decisions. Many – although not of course all – of the benefits of decision analysis will then still be realised.

Table 6.10

Advantages and disadvantages of decision analysis

Advantages	Disadvantages
The decision maker is forced to come to quantitative grips with the problem.	Some outcomes cannot be quantified in monetary terms.
The decision maker is forced to distinguish between the attractiveness of outcomes and their chance of occurring.	Managers are often unwilling to commit themselves by providing subjective probabilities.
The judgements of different experts within a company can be combined on a tree.	Decision trees are apt to become 'bushy' very quickly and the manager must exercise judgement in deciding which branches to consider.
The tree is a focus for discussion: if two executives disagree it enables their reason for disagreement to be pinpointed.	Often a continuous spectrum of different events has to be split into discrete possibilities (e.g. sales levels).
The value of information is considered explicitly.	Decisions are often made for political reasons and the decision tree may become a 'political pawn'.
The important uncertainties are distinguished from the unimportant ones.	

References

Further reading

Brown, R.V., Kahr, A.S. and Peterson, C., *Decision Analysis for the Manager,* Holt Reinhart and Winston, 1974.

Magee, J.R., 'Decision Trees for Decision Making', *Harvard Business Review,* July–August 1964, pp. 126–38.

Moore, P.G., *Risk in Business Decision,* London Business School Series, 1972.

Raiffa, H., *Decision Analysis: Introductory Lectures on Choice Under Uncertainty,* Addison Wesley, 1968.

Thomas, H., *Decision Theory and the Manager,* Pitman, London 1972.

Applications

Beattie, D.W., 'Marketing a New Product', *Operational Research Quarterly,* vol. 20, no. 4, 1969, pp. 429–35.

Franks, J.R., Bunton, C.J. and Broyles, J.E., 'A Decision Analysis Approach to Cash Flow Management', *Operational Research Quarterly,* vol. 24, no. 4, December 1974.

Grayson, C.J., *Decision Under Uncertainty: Drilling Decisions by Oil and Gas Operators,* Harvard Business School, Division of Research, 1960.

Longbottom, D.A., 'The Application of Decision Analysis to a New Product Planning Decision', *Operational Research Quarterly,* vol. 24, 1973, pp. 9–17.

Magee, J.F., 'How to Use Decision Trees in Capital Investment', *Harvard Business Review,* September–October 1964, pp. 79–96.

Exercises

1 The probabilities that a certain piece of equipment will require repair 0, 1, 2 and 3 times in a year are 0·1, 0·5, 0·3, 0·1 respectively. The cost of one repair is £20. What is the expected cost per year?

2 A local authority's usage of mechanical diggers varies from day to day. On some days it uses none at all; on others it can use as many as three. The following costs have been worked out:
Cost of owning but not using digger per day = £20 (mainly depreciation).
Cost of owning and using digger per day = £40.
Cost of hiring a digger from a plant hire company = £50 per day.

From past data it is estimated that the probabilities of 0, 1, 2, 3 diggers being required in a day are 0·1, 0·4, 0·3 and 0·2 respectively. How many diggers should the authority own?

3 The decision in exercise 2 might be said to be fundamentally different from the one confronting the aircraft manufacturer considered in this chapter in that the payoff occurs many times, not just once. How appropriate do you think EMV is in the two situations?

157

4   A card shop owner is trying to decide how many boxes of an expensive Mother's Day card to stock. The cards carry a high profit margin and come in boxes of 20; they cost £1·60 and retail for £2·70. Each box unsold by Mother's Day can be sold afterwards for £1·20. 0·1, 0·2, 0·4, 0·2 and 0·1 are the probabilities of 0, 1, 2, 3, 4 boxes being demanded. How many boxes should the owner stock at the beginning of the season if it is impossible to place re-orders? (Ignore the possibility of only part of a box being sold.)

5   How could the interest which the retailer earns on money not invested in cards be taken into account in exercise 4?

6   An oil prospecting company has an option to drill for oil on a certain piece of land. The option is open for a limited period only, and is shortly due to expire. It will cost the company £100,000 to undertake exploratory drilling work, and this money will, of course, be wasted if no oil is found. It is by no means certain that oil is present. The company geologist estimates subjectively that the probability of oil being present in commercial quantities is 0·55. If oil is found, the company will sell the development rights for £400,000.

   Before committing themselves to drilling, the company has the opportunity to carry out seismic tests at a cost of £30,000 to provide more information about whether or not oil is likely to be found. From previous situations in which these tests have been used, it is known that if the test results are favourable, there is a probability of 0·85 that oil is present. If, however, the test results are unfavourable, there is a probability of only 0·10 that oil could be present.

   Should the company go ahead immediately with drilling operations, carry out seismic tests first, or let the option expire without taking any action?

(The probability that the seismic tests will give a favourable result is required in the analysis. This may be deduced as 0·60 from the probabilities already given.)

7   A development project involving the use of a new adhesive in shoe manufacture can be described (in simplified form) as occupying two stages.

   (i)   Laboratory development of the adhesive to meet a set of requirements as laid down by the product development committee.
   (ii) Transfer of the use of the adhesive (if successful) from the laboratory to production.

Stage (i) may take two or four months (intermediate durations are not considered).

Examination of research records of similar projects show that 30 per cent of such products are transferred to production at the end of two months and 40 per cent are screened out as impracticable at the end of two months. Of the remaining 30 per cent, half were successful in the sense that they could be transferred to production at the end of four months.

The cost of laboratory development work for this project is estimated at £1,000 per month. If the adhesive is transferred to production there is an 80 per cent probability of it being incorporated successfully, and this outcome is worth £20,000 in present value terms. There is a 20 per cent chance of such an adhesive being incorporated unsuccessfully if it reaches the production stage. The cost of an abortive attempt to incorporate a product which had appeared successfully in development would be about £5,000.

Should the company embark on such a project? Examine the possible decisions in detail.

8   Bulls Bros is a small firm of building contractors currently making a profit of £10,000 per annum and concentrating on relatively small jobs (each lasting between one and three months). Although there is no shortage of this type of work the directors would like at some stage to start undertaking bigger (potentially more profitable) contracts. There are two possibilities:

(i)   The cinema contract (one year's duration): Tenders for this must be submitted this month and the winner will be announced at the end of the month.

(ii)   The supermarket contract (one year's duration): This is potentially more profitable to Bulls than the cinema contract. Tenders must be submitted next month and the winner will be announced at the end of that month.

Either contract, if won, would be started in three months' time and would tie up the company's resources to such an extent that it would be unable to bid for or to undertake any other work for a whole year after that. In particular, if Bulls won the cinema contract, it would be unable to bid for the supermarket contract.

The company has assessed its probability of winning either contract with a 'high' tender as 0·2 and with a 'low' tender as 0·7. Profits are estimated as follows:

	Cinema contract	Supermarket contract
High tender	£50,000	£80,000
Low tender	£20,000	£40,000

Draw a decision tree of the situation facing Bulls and recommend a course of action. What is the expected profit from the course of action which you recommend?

9   What is the expected value of perfect information in the case of the aircraft manufacturer considered on p. 137. How can this be interpreted?

10   Some time ago Consolidated Chemicals agreed to supply Morgan Manufacturers with a batch of a rare chemical reagent: PQ–73. The contract drawn up between the two companies included two penalty clauses:

(i)   A penalty of £20,000 in the event of late delivery.
(ii)   A penalty of £50,000 in the event of the PQ–73 being substandard and ruining Morgan's production process.

This morning, just as he was about to ship the batch to Morgans, the production manager of Consolidated learnt that his supplies of an important constituent chemical of PQ–73 might have become contaminated and that the batch of PQ–73 already produced might therefore be substandard. He assessed the probability of this to be 0·2.

Instead of shipping the batch as planned, the production manager can decide to scrap it and to attempt to produce another batch (which he is certain would be up to the required standard) in time to meet Morgan's deadline. Working normal time on this second batch would cost £4,000 and give a 50 per cent chance of the batch being ready for shipment within a week. Working overtime would cost £6,000 and give a 90 per cent chance of this. In either case it is certain that this second batch would be ready for shipment within two weeks.

Experts estimate that there is a 90 per cent chance of a batch of PQ–73 reaching Morgans on time if it is shipped by sea now; 70 per cent if it is shipped by sea within the next week; 50 per cent if it is shipped by sea within the week after next. However, at any time right up to the last minute the decision to ship by air can be taken. This would cost £8,000 more than shipping by sea, but would ensure delivery on time.

Draw a decision tree of the situation facing Consolidated and recommend a course of action. How sensitive is this recommendation to the probability of the batch being substandard? What is the value of perfect information on whether the batch is substandard? How can this perfect information be interpreted?

11   An oil wildcatter must decide whether to drill at a given site before his option expires. The cost of drilling is £70,000 and if the hole is dry there will be no return. If it is wet the return will be £120,000 (giving a net profit of £50,000) and if it is soaking the net profit will be £200,000.

At a cost of £10,000 the wildcatter can take seismic soundings which will help determine the underlying geological structure. Experts have provided the following table of probabilities.

	No structure	Open structure	Closed structure
Dry	0·30	0·15	0·05
Wet	0·09	0·12	0·09
Soaking	0·02	0·08	0·10

The table indicates that, for example, the probability of both no structure and a wet hole is 0·09 etc.

(a)   Assuming the wildcatter uses EMV as his decision criterion, what is his best course of action?

(b)   What is the expected value of perfect information?

(c)   What is the expected value of seismic information?

12   Experience shows that a certain production process producing fibre-glass reinforcement on an electro-mechanical structure is liable to fail in service, due to defects in the setting of the fibreglass. Records of subsequent performance in service show that 20 per cent of the re-inforcements are defective in this way.

A not too satisfactory test is available to detect such defects before dispatch of the product. Laboratory trials of the testing device indicate that it has only a 90 per cent chance of detecting a fibreglass reinforcement which is faulty. Also, it has a 15 per cent chance of indicating that a reinforcement is faulty when in fact it is sound.

Calculate the probability of fibreglass reinforcements failing in service if no faults are detected by the testing device.

13   A company has manufactured a special guidance system for a small satellite earth station, and the system has passed its normal customer-witnessed works tests. Previous experience indicates that 25 per cent of

such installations suffer from instability due to problems in the design of the feed-back mechanism, and these problems become apparent when the equipment is installed on site. Rectification of such faults once the equipment is installed is expensive. Installation and commissioning is additionally subject to teething troubles of a more general kind and this occurs in about 50 per cent of installations of this type.

Site installation costs are roughly as follows, depending on how much difficulty arises on site.

Trouble free installation:	£7,000
Installation with only teething troubles:	£11,000
Installation with instability only:	£17,000
Installation with instability and teething troubles:	£21,000

There is a suggestion that the equipment be set up for a pre-installation trial, additional to the works test, using a field at the bottom of the car park. The cost of such trials would be £2,500. If such trials were undertaken there is a 0·8 probability that an unstable guidance system would be revealed by the tests, in which case rectification would be undertaken in the works at a cost of £5,000. There would then be a 50/50 chance between a trouble-free installation and teething troubles on site. On the other hand, supposing the equipment was free from instability, there is a chance the trials could erroneously indicate instability due to ghosting from a nearby railway track. There is about a 0·1 probability of this happening with an installation which has no real instability.

Draw out an appropriate decision tree and recommend whether or not the suggested pre-installation trial should be adopted.

14 You are charged with the inventory control job in the Volant Manufacturing Company. You think there is about a 0·4 chance of a recession next year. If there is a recession next year, you should sell the AE4 model now for the last-offer price of $1 million, because you could get only $800,000 for it in a recession year. These amounts would be received in one year. However, you have a promise from the purchasing agent of a leading company to buy AE4 for $1·3 million if there is no recession (amount payable one year hence). After some preliminary calculations, you are still undecided about selling, and determined to gather evidence about the chances of a recession next year. You discover that bad debts have been rising recently. A little investigation indicates that, for the last ten recessions, bad debts started to increase approximately a year early in eight instances. You are willing to accept 0·8 as an estimate of the probability of bad debts

rising, given that a recession will occur a year later. In the same sense, you find that, for ten randomly selected normal years, the economy experienced rising bad debts the previous year in three instances. Thus, you take 0·3 as an estimate of P (rising bad debts/no recession next year). If you revise your prior probabilities according to the Bayes theorem, what would you do about the AE4?

Case E   Corsair Chemicals

Background

In the mid-1970s Corsair Chemicals was a medium-sized British manufacturer of industrial chemical products. Its turnover was in the region of
£50 million per annum (40 per cent of which was accounted for by
exports) and it owned plants at three different locations within the UK.
The company had five directors:

Joe Rydall (Managing Director)
Peter Boyd (R and D Director)
John Garnett (Production Director)
Colin Hooks (Finance Director)
Alan Rayburn (Marketing Director)

Their average age was 49.

The Baritex problem

On 11 March 1976 Corsair's directors met to discuss the possibility of
making use of some research recently carried out by Peter Boyd's
department into new methods of producing a polymer, known as Baritex.
The dialogue which follows is an extract from their discussions.

Joe Rydall: Let me start by summarising the position as I see it. As you
    all know, up to now we haven't considered it worth while to produce
    Baritex ourselves. This is because the total world market is not all that
    great and we've always thought that the large capital outlays on plant
    could not really be justified. Now the situation is different. Last
    December Peter's department made what I can only describe as a
    remarkable discovery. It found a brand new way of producing
    Baritex in commercial quantities which is quite different from that
    currently being used by the big German and American firms. Today's
    meeting has been called to discuss how we can best take advantage
    of the situation. Peter, perhaps you'd like to start.

Peter Boyd: Yes, thank you. I don't think there's any need for me to go
    into any of the technical details. You've all got a copy of my report
    anyway. The main point is, I think, that not only is this a new way
    of producing Baritex, it's also a far cheaper way. My department
    estimates that it cuts the unit cost of production from £200 per ton
    to £120 per ton.

Joe Rydall: Alan, I believe you've got some figures on the size of the Baritex market.

Alan Rayburn: Yes. Unfortunately they're all very approximate. The total world market is, I estimate, in the region of 20,000 tons per annum.

Joe Rydall: And how much of that could we hope to get?

Alan Rayburn: Well, at the moment the market is dominated by the German firm, Moche, and the American firm, Transchem. I've summarised the position as I see it on this sheet. *(distributes Exhibit 1)* As I said before, my figures are only very approximate. You see first of all a rough breakdown of the total market into regions: 1,000 tons for the UK, 4,000 tons for the rest of Europe and so on. The price being charged at the moment is around £400 per ton. If we charged this, my guess is that we'd sell between 500 and 1,500 tons per year, but as the price goes down, of course . . .

Peter Boyd: Have you considered the possibility that the total size of the market may actually depend on price?

Alan Rayburn: Yes, I have. The market's probably a little price elastic, but it's difficult to be sure about that. My figures for the size of Corsair's market are all based on a fixed total world market of 20,000 tons and in that sense, I suppose, they are conservative.

Joe Rydall: Well, working on the basis of Peter's unit cost figure of £120 per ton we shouldn't have to charge more than £250 per ton. It looks as though we need a plant capable of producing at least 3,000 tons per year.

Peter Boyd: Yes, I'd go along with that.

John Garnett: The thing that worries me, Peter, is that you've only shown that your new method for producing Baritex works in the lab. You know as well as I do that we may hit all sorts of snags when we try to produce the stuff in commercial quantities and that the final unit cost may be way above £120 per ton. It seems to me that you should carry out more tests before we commit ourselves.

Peter Boyd: Yes, John, but the tests would take about a year to complete; they'd be expensive and even when we'd carried them out we still wouldn't be exactly certain what our unit costs were going to be. I agree with you that my unit cost figure may prove to be a little optimistic, but we're not talking about a tremendous sum of money. I think we can afford to take the risk and build a plant now.

Joe Rydall: Colin, what do you think about all this? I believe you've carried out some financial analyses.

Colin Hooks: Well, my department is actually carrying out detailed financial analyses at the moment, but to give you an idea of the sort of sums of money we're talking about I produced this. (*distributes Exhibit 2*) It looks at two possibilities. The first one involves building a plant capable of producing 1,000 tons per annum, the second involves a plant capable of producing 3,000 tons per annum. In both cases I've assumed that we operate at full capacity, sell at £250 per ton and have a unit cost of £120 per ton. As you can see we do get quite a few economies of scale with the 3,000 ton plant.

John Garnett: Yes, but a 3,000 ton plant is more risky. If we insist on going ahead now I'd rather settle for a 1,000 ton plant. We can always extend it later.

Joe Rydall: Yes, but doing it that way always costs more in the long run. Colin, have you estimated how much extra it would cost if we built a 1,000 ton plant and then extended it to 3,000 tons later?

Colin Hooks: If past experience is anything to go by, I suppose the extension would cost us about an extra £150,000 at today's prices.

Joe Rydall: And, Peter, what about the cost of your department carrying out further research along the lines John suggests?

Peter Boyd: About £50,000 – but of course we'd lose a year's sales as well.

Assignment

Draw a decision tree describing the situation facing Corsair Chemicals. What further information would you require before recommending a course of action to Joe Rydall?

Exhibit 1

Summary of Baritex market, March 1976

Total market size (tons per annum): 20,000
Price per ton (£)   : 400–410

Analysis of world market:

Region	Tons per annum
UK	1,000
Rest of Europe	4,000
N. America	10,000
Rest of world	5,000

Estimates of size of Corsair's market for different prices:

Price (£)	Market size (tons per annum)
400	500–1,500
350	1,000–2,000
300	2,000–3,000
250	3,000–4,000

Exhibit 2

Brief financial analyses re Baritex

The following figures must be regarded as very approximate. They ignore working capital requirements, taxation, the effects of discounting etc. The cost price is assumed to be £120 per ton and the selling price £250 per ton. Five years are considered.

Case 1 – 1,000 ton plant

	£'000s
Initial investment	150
Total variable costs (5 years)	600
Total fixed costs (5 years)	150
Revenue from sales (5 years)	1,250
Net cash flow over 5 year period:	£350,000

Case 2 – 3,000 ton plant

	£'000s
Initial investment	250
Total variable costs (5 years)	1,800
Total fixed costs (5 years)	200
Revenue from sales (5 years)	3,750
Net cash flow over 5 year period:	£1,500,000

7 Using models successfully

In this book a number of quantitative problem-solving techniques have been introduced. Some companies have applied these techniques with considerable success; others have achieved only limited success. In this chapter we shall look at the difficulties which can arise in the application of the techniques and the ways in which these difficulties can be overcome.

Reasons for failure

An analysis of cases where model building has been unsuccessful reveals a consistent pattern of reasons for failure.

Inadequate management support

In many cases where the introduction of operational research into an organisation has failed, top management have been either neutral or luke-warm in their support. Usually operational research has been introduced on the recommendation of consultants or at the request of a middle manager, without senior management feeling committed to its success. This can create two sorts of problems. First it may result in the operational research function reporting at too low a level. This can cause difficulties if a conflict arises, as the reporting manager may not be senior enough to resolve it. Also this will restrict the scope of the investigation carried out, as the reporting manager may not have the authority to allow the investigators to question company policy decisions. Secondly, if senior management do not give a high priority to operational research and do not actively support its introduction then lower levels of management will do the same. Managers will be less willing to give full co-operation to the operational researchers so that their investigations will be less effective. This will have a cumulative effect as the ineffectiveness of early investigations will make managers even less willing to commit their own time and that of their staff to assisting the operational researchers. Eventually the operational research department will be closed down due to its lack of success or because the staff have become frustrated and moved to other jobs.

Poor human relations

Another major cause of failure has been poor communication between the operational research team and management. This problem of communications has been particularly pronounced when the background of managers and operational researchers has been widely different. In organisations where managers are short on qualifications but long on experience and used to managing by gut feel, the managers are naturally hostile to the operational research approach. They see the operational researchers as young whizz kids who have no knowledge of the industry and are telling experienced managers how they should do their job. The operational researchers on the other hand, see the managers as blind to new ideas and unwilling to contemplate any change in their methods of operation. As a result of this antagonism, co-operation is difficult so that the operational researchers end up by collecting their data and reaching their conclusions independently of operating management. This means that as the managers have not participated in the investigation they feel in no way committed to the successful implementation of its recommendations. Also the investigators will not have made use of the extremely valuable experience and judgement of the managers. The authors know of one situation where the operational research department produced a report recommending a procedure which looked excellent on paper, but which could not be introduced because it involved a totally unacceptable transfer of work between unions. If there had been more management involvement in the early stages of the investigation, a great deal of the department's time could have been saved.

Insufficient allowance for operating staff

There is an unfortunate tendency for operational researchers to design a new procedure without any consideration of the people who will operate it. If it is too complex for the operating staff to understand then they are likely to make errors, leading the procedure into disrepute. Also, if the procedure is too complex for the decision maker to understand then he is unlikely to agree to its introduction.

Inappropriate use of techniques

Operational research should be essentially problem-orientated. The solution techniques which are used are an important but subsidiary part of the total problem-solving process. Some investigators, however, become dedicated to the application of the techniques for their own sake. One investigator will formulate every problem as a linear program, another tries to solve every problem using simulation. Where inappropriate techniques are used it is likely that the recommendations made will also be inappropriate.

Another related problem is the tendency for some operational research teams to continue an investigation to the point where the cost of the investigation exceeds the potential benefits. Any operational research department whose running costs exceed the savings it generates is unlikely to have a very long life.

Ignoring factors which are difficult to quantify

When constructing a model, inevitably simplifications must be made in order to reduce the time taken in constructing the model and in order to make the model amenable to solution. Factors which are left out will tend to be those which are intangible or difficult to quantify. Such factors include the effect of a change in working methods on staff morale and the effect of a change in product range on sales. These factors are often very important and must be taken account of if only in a very informal way; otherwise actual results may be considerably different from those predicted. One bus company carried out a major routing exercise and as a result closed down a number of its routes and started several new ones. The company believed that this would lead to a substantial reduction in total costs while still maintaining the same level of service. They did not take full account of the resistance to change of existing bus users. As a result of public pressure one of the closed routes had to be started up again. This wiped out most of the predicted savings.

Requirements for success

We have looked at the factors contributing to the failure of operational research in organisations. What can management do when introducing operational research in their own organisations in order to give it the greatest chance of success?

Top management support

A major requirement for success is the active and enthusiastic support of top management. Preferably the recommendation to introduce operational research should come from a member of top management. He will then encourage the use of operational research by other senior managers and defend the operational research team should the need arise.

Involve managers in the investigations

Ideally operational research staff will combine technical ability with management experience so that they have an understanding of managerial problems. They should also be good at communicating their ideas to management and discussing common problems on an equal footing. Each investigating team will of course include one or more specialist operational research staff. The team should also include members of operating management from the area being investigated, on either a full-time or a part-time basis. Their experience will be invaluable during the investigation. They will shorten the data collection stage by knowing the best place to obtain necessary information, they will be able to ensure that the model includes all the key variables and constraints and they will be able to judge whether the final recommendations are practical.

Even managers who are not included in the investigating team should be kept fully informed of progress at every stage in the investigation. Not only will each manager have the opportunity to point out important factors which have been omitted and potential practical problems, but also each manager will feel involved in the investigation and therefore committed to its success.

Careful selection of initial projects

It is vitally important that the first few projects tackled using operational research in an organisation are seen to be successful. Once operational research has shown that it can yield tangible benefits, managers will be more willing to ask for operational research assistance with their own problems. The first projects selected should therefore be investigations which are thought to have a high probability of success and where the payoff will be quick and easily measurable.

In one engineering company the first project tackled by operational research was an investigation into the scheduling of work on to machines. This was a major problem area, with poor production control leading to low machine utilisation and a high proportion of late orders. The company had tried to solve the problem by recruiting more progress chasers, but this only meant that there were more men fighting over the same machines and the situation deteriorated further. The operational research team concentrated their attention on solutions which could be rapidly implemented. They devised a new method of manual scheduling which could be introduced immediately. This produced a substantial improvement in the number of orders completed on time and led to a reduction in the number of progress chasers employed. Some time later the team carried out a further investigation which resulted in the whole production control system being computerised. This was extremely successful but implementation took a lot of time and effort. It would have been unwise to have undertaken such a large and complex project until operational research had proved its usefulness with a number of smaller scale projects.

Involve investigators in implementation

A fault of many operational research projects is that the involvement of the investigators stops once the final report has been presented. The argument for this is that operating management will be much better at handling the practical problems of implementation. Also they will have to live with the new system and so they have a powerful incentive to make sure it works smoothly from the start.

Certainly operating management must be involved in implementation, but the operational researchers should be equally involved. A number of unforeseen problems will arise which may require modifications to the model and hence to the final solution. This can only be done by the operational research staff. Also the operational research staff will become much more aware of the problems which arise when converting a new procedure from theory into practice. This should mean that in future investigations operational research staff will produce more realistic and workable solutions.

Concentrate on problems not techniques

Many operational researchers start with a technique and then look round for a problem to apply it to. In order to do this the problem is often modified to fit the technique instead of the technique being modified to fit the problem. In order to ensure that the emphasis is on solving problems rather than on applying techniques, it is important that management are very much involved in the recognition and definition of problems. Management should carry out a full survey to identify problem areas where performance could be improved and the decisions which are crucial to the future well-being of the organisation. Operational staff could assist by carrying out a feasibility study on each problem identified, indicating the potential benefits, the cost of the investigation, the time it would take and the probability of success. It should then be possible to prepare a forward programme of investigation which could be revised at intervals as conditions change and more pressing problems arise.

The use of a problem-solving approach will mean that many investigations will not require the traditional techniques of operational research at all. They will be soluble using simple statistics or elementary logic. This may be frustrating for the investigator who enjoys constructing complicated mathematical models, but the real operational researcher gets his satisfaction from the challenge of solving difficult problems by whatever means is most suitable.

Aim for simplicity of operation

While the model and the method of solution used in an investigation may be extremely complicated, the final recommendation should be kept as simple as possible. If a new procedure is to be installed then full account must be taken of the calibre of the staff who will be operating it. In some cases it may be necessary to simplify some of the decision rules, even if this means a slight reduction in effectiveness, in order to reduce the chance of misinterpretation. In other cases it may be preferable to introduce a new procedure in several phases, starting with a very simple procedure and introducing additional features as staff become familiar with the new approach. Also a lot of attention should be paid to making the procedure easy to use by providing tables, decision charts and other devices to simplify the operation of the procedure.

Make sure people are fully informed

Right from the start of an investigation it is important that everyone in the departments involved understands what is happening and why the investigation is necessary. In order to ensure full co-operation at every level all should be aware of the benefits which are likely to result from the investigation. Also, any fears about job security or reduction in status should be allayed if possible.

In order that managers can properly assist the investigators, they need to be aware of the approach and methods being used. This can be achieved by holding a series of seminars on operational research, run by the operational research staff.

When the investigation has been completed and its recommendations accepted it is important that the staff who will be affected by the changes understand the new procedures which are to be introduced and the reasons for their introduction. Frequently a hand simulation of the operation of the system using the new procedure will be useful. It can be used both to demonstrate how the new procedure will operate and to train staff in its use.

173

The benefits of using models

In this book we have emphasised the use of quantitative models to assist in management problem-solving and decision making. What are the special benefits of using models rather than relying entirely on the judgement and experience of the managers concerned? Obviously judgement and experience will always be important factors, but we believe that quantitative models can be used to provide valuable additional information on which the manager can exercise his judgement. The benefits of the model building approach are as follows:

Better solutions

The use of quantitative models will usually lead to better solutions, especially with problems which involve a number of inter-related variables. The human brain is not very good at handling more than one variable at a time, and so it can only deal with multiple variable problems by making a large number of simplifications and assumptions. These assumptions are particularly dangerous as they are unlikely to be made explicit. Models, on the other hand, are ideally suited to dealing with multiple variable problems. Some assumptions and simplifications will still be necessary, but they will be considerably less than for the human brain and they will be clearly stated.

Longer term solutions

Most management decisions are taken in order to deal with an immediate crisis. When the same problem arises again in a different context a new decision must be made, usually at a fairly senior level of management. Using a model it is frequently possible to develop a general set of decision rules which can be applied not only to the immediate problem but to any similar problems which may arise in the future. Once a decision has been reduced to an objective and routine basis, it can in future be dealt with at a much lower level in the organisation, freeing senior management to concentrate on those problems which cannot be handled in this way.

Even in situations where conditions change dramatically so that existing decision rules are no longer valid, it is usually relatively simple to update the model. The revised model can then be used to produce a modified set of decision rules.

More precise problem definition

The formal model building approach forces managers to think in quantitative terms about the problem being investigated. Precise objectives must be specified. The key variables must be specified. Any constraints on the problem must be stated. In defining the problem in such precise terms the manager clarifies his own thinking about the problem and is therefore likely to reach a better final decision.

Objective analysis

Decisions based on management judgement can be very subjective. When problems involve more than one department or functional area, then different managers will suggest different courses of action depending on their own point of view and special interests. A model building approach can provide an objective analysis which incorporates the special requirements of each functional area leading to a solution which best meets the objectives of the organisation as a whole.

Index

The authors

John Hull has worked for the British Shoe Corporation as a Corporate Planner and has been a Senior Research Officer at the London Business School. Since 1972 he has lectured on Quantitative Aspects of Management at Cranfield School of Management.

John Mapes has alternately worked in industry and lectured. He has held posts with ICI and Clayton Dewandre Ltd, and has lectured at the Hendon College of Technology. He has been a Lecturer in Quantitative Aspects of Management at Cranfield School of Management since 1971.

Brian Wheeler was previously Senior Mechanical Engineer at Brush Electrical Engineering Co. Ltd. He has lectured at Loughborough University, and has been a lecturer in the Quantitative Aspects of Management at Cranfield School of Management since 1969.

Other SAXON HOUSE publications

Hodges, M.	*Multinational corporations and national governments*
Liggins, D.	*National economic planning in France*
Friedly, P. H.	*National policy responses to urban growth*
Madelin, H.	*Oil and politics*
Tilford, R. (ed.)	*The Ostpolitik and political change in Germany*
Friedrichs, J., H. Ludtke	*Participant observation*
Fitzmaurice, J.	*The party groups in the European parliament*
Brown, J., G. Howes (eds)	*The police and the community*
Lang, R. W.	*The politics of drugs*
Denton, F. T., B. G. Spencer	*Population and the economy*
Dickinson, J. P. (ed.)	*Portfolio analysis*
Wilson, D. J.	*Power and party bureaucracy in Britain*
Wabe, J. S.	*Problems in manpower forecasting*
Willis, K. G.	*Problems in migration analysis*
Farnsworth, R. A.	*Productivity and law*
Shepherd, R. J.	*Public opinion and European integration*
Richardson, H. W.	*Regional development policy and planning in Spain*
Sant, M. (ed.)	*Regional policy and planning for Europe*
Thorpe, D. (ed.)	*Research into retailing and distribution*
Dickinson, J. P.	*Risk and uncertainty in accounting and finance*
Hey, R. D., T. D. Davies (eds)	*Science, technology and environmental management*
Britton, D. K., B. Hill	*Size and efficiency in farming*
Buchholz, E., et al	*Socialist criminology*
Paterson, W. E.	*The SPD and European integration*
Blohm, H., K. Steinbuch (eds)	*Technological forecasting in practice*
Piepe, A., et al	*Television and the working class*
Goodhardt, G. J., et al	*The television audience*
May, T. C.	*Trade unions and pressure group politics*
Labini, P. S.	*Trade unions, inflation and productivity*
Casadio, G. P.	*Transatlantic trade*
Whitehead, C. M. E.	*The U.K. housing market*
Balfour, C.	*Unions and the law*